W9-CTO-086

Canadian Labour in Crisis

Compliments of
www.fernwoodpublishing.ca
__exam copy to:_____$_____
_V_ review copy to: Steve $19.95
Early

Canadian Labour in Crisis

Reinventing the Workers' Movement

David Camfield

Fernwood Publishing • Halifax & Winnipeg

Copyright © 2011 David Camfield

All rights reserved. No part of this book may be reproduced or transmitted in
any form by any means without permission in writing from the publisher,
except by a reviewer, who may quote brief passages in a review.

Editing: Tara Seel
Cover Design: John van der Woude
Printed and bound in Canada by Hignell Book Printing

MIX
Paper from
responsible sources
FSC® C013916

Published in Canada by Fernwood Publishing
32 Oceanvista Lane
Black Point, Nova Scotia, B0J 1B0
and 748 Broadway Avenue, Winnipeg, Manitoba, R3G 0X3
www.fernwoodpublishing.ca

Fernwood Publishing Company Limited gratefully acknowledges the financial support of the
Government of Canada through the Canada Book Fund, the Canada Council for the Arts,
the Nova Scotia Department of Tourism and Culture, the Manitoba Department of Culture,
Heritage and Tourism under the Manitoba Publishers Marketing Assistance Program
and the Province of Manitoba, through the Book Publishing Tax Credit,
for our publishing program.

Library and Archives Canada Cataloguing in Publication

Camfield, David
Canadian labour in crisis : reinventing the workers' movement / David
Camfield.

Includes bibliographical references and index.
ISBN 978-1-55266-416-2

1. Labor movement--Canada. 2. Labor unions--Canada. 3. Working
class--Canada--Political activity. 4. Working class--Canada--Social
conditions. I. Title.

HD8104.C33 2011   331.0971   C2010-908048-3

Contents

Acknowledgments

I owe an enormous debt to many union members and staffers and community activists with whom I have talked and worked over the last two decades, including those who agreed to be interviewed or who corresponded with me during my research for this book (not all of whom are quoted or cited with respect to specific points and therefore appear in the endnotes). I have learned a great deal from them.

For providing me with material during the research and writing of this book or for responding to inquiries, I thank Sebastien Bouchard; Robert Comeau; Karl Flecker; Xavier Lafrance; Katherine Nastovski; Jeff Noonan; Jean-Marc Piotte; Sheila Wilmot; staff at the Strategic Policy, Analysis, and Workplace Information Directorate of Human Resources and Skills Development Canada; and several individuals who will remain anonymous (apologies to anyone I have forgotten here). Kim Parry, Aviva Cipilinski and Krista Walters ably transcribed recordings of research interviews. A grant from the Global Political Economy Research Fund at the University of Manitoba helped me to travel to conduct interviews. University of Toronto Press granted permission to use material drawn from my chapter "The Working-Class Movement in Canada: An Overview" in *Group Politics and Social Movements in Canada*, edited by Miriam Smith.

For comments on drafts of this book, I must thank Brian McDougall, David McNally, Alan Sears, Sheila Wilmot, Monique Woroniak and two anonymous reviewers for Fernwood. I am grateful to Alan and Sheila for lively discussions in recent years about issues addressed in this book. Monique has made my life so much better, and helped keep my life in balance during the sabbatical in which this book was written.

At Fernwood, Wayne Antony responded enthusiastically to my book proposal. My editor, Jessica Antony, was a pleasure to work with. Thanks to Beverley Rach, Nancy Malek, Tara Seel and Debbie Mathers for bringing the book through to publication.

Finally, I must thank my parents, Adrian and Jennifer Camfield, for instilling in me as a child a love of reading and respect for writing that set me on the path towards this book. In recognition of that gift, I dedicate it to them.

Acronyms

BCNU: British Columbia Nurses' Union

BCTF: British Columbia Teachers' Federation

CAW: Canadian Auto Workers (formally the National Automobile, Aerospace, Transportation and General Workers Union of Canada)

CCF: Cooperative Commonwealth Federation

CEP: Communication, Energy and Paperworkers' Union

CLC: Canadian Labour Congress

CPC: Communist Party of Canada

CSN: Confédération des Syndicats Nationaux (Confederation of National Trade Unions)

CUPE: Canadian Union of Public Employees

CUPW: Canadian Union of Postal Workers

FIQ: Fédération Interprofessionnelle de la Santé du Québec

HERE: Hotel Employees, Restaurant Employees International Union

HEU: Hospital Employees' Union

IWC: Immigrant Workers' Centre

NDP: New Democratic Party

NOII: No One Is Illegal

OCAP: Ontario Coalition Against Poverty

SEIU: Service Employees' International Union

TINA: There Is No Alternative

TWU: Telecommunication Workers' Union

TYRLC: Toronto and York Region Labour Council

UFCW: United Food and Commercial Workers'

UNITE: United Needletrades, Industrial and Textile Employees

UNITE HERE: The union created by the merger of UNITE and HERE in 2004 (not an acronym)

USW: United Steel Workers (formally the United Steel, Paper and Forestry, Rubber, Manufacturing, Energy, Allied-Industrial and Service Workers' International Union)

WAC: Workers' Action Centre

Introduction

"There's a workers' movement in Canada? Really? It sure doesn't feel like it." This is how many people would probably respond to finding out what this book is about. Yet the website of the Canadian Labour Congress (CLC), the main federation of unions and the biggest umbrella organization of the working-class movement, claims it is "the largest democratic and popular organization in Canada with over three million members."[1] People sometimes refer to unions as "the labour movement." Why most of the unions that belong to the CLC (like other unions) do not feel much like a movement to most people is one of the questions this book sets out to answer. But before we can examine the working-class movement, we need to take a look at the working class.

The Working Class?

One of the most significant sources of confusion in looking at anything to do with class in Canada and Quebec[2] is that most people who are part of the working class do not think of themselves as such. Most people assume they belong to the middle class — people "in the middle" — in between the small rich elite and people who live in poverty (Seccombe and Livingstone 2000: 59–61). The term "working class" is often associated only with people (usually men) who work in "blue collar" jobs in manufacturing, construction or transportation. But there is a different way of looking at class that more accurately captures how the social structure of the capitalist society we live in is organized.

From this alternative perspective, most people in our society are part of the working class.[3] Everyone who sells their ability to work to an employer in exchange for a wage (whether this is paid in the form of an hourly wage or a salary) and who does not wield truly substantial management authority is part of the working class. This is the case regardless of how much they are paid or how much autonomy they have at work.[4] Unemployed wage-earners are also part of the working class. So too are the unwaged people who live in households that depend on wage income, such as people (mostly women) who work as unpaid caregivers at home. All these people are part of the working class because they share *a common relationship both to the way society is organized to produce goods and services and to other classes in society*, especially the class of employers. That relationship — between people who sell their ability to work in exchange for wages, on the one hand, and employers on the other — is the central class relation in our society.

The specific kinds of work that people are employed to do changes over time. For example, in the early twenty-first century, the proportion of people who work in factories or as domestic servants in Canada and Quebec is much lower than it was a century ago, while a much larger proportion of people work in office jobs. But the specific kind of work people are hired to do is not the issue here. Nor is their status in society, what they think about their class position, how much money they make or how many years of formal education they have. None of these things determine whether or not someone is part of the working class (though they do influence how people act and think, so of course they matter).[5] What determines the class someone belongs to is their place in the whole system of production. *What people in the working class have in common is that they do not own or control society's means of producing goods and services* (factories, farms, mines, offices, schools, hospitals and so on) *and so they are forced to try to sell their ability to work to those who do* (or to depend on people who are forced to work for wages, in the case of unwaged people in the households of wage-earners).

The working class, then, is much broader and more diverse than is usually thought. Today it includes both high-paid miners and retail staff who make minimum wage. It includes computer game designers (mostly white men) and support workers in health care (mostly women, many of them women of colour). It encompasses citizens and non-citizens. It includes people who work for pay for thirty-five hours a week at one job and do little unpaid work in the household, and others who work for wages part-time on top of long hours of unpaid work taking care of children in the home. In this book, "worker" refers to any member of the working class, whether they are currently working for wages or not.

Many people who are usually thought of as "middle class" — such as nurses, teachers and IT specialists — are, in fact, part of the working class, including many people who have "manager" in their job title. However, employers and self-employed people, such as doctors, lawyers and consultants, are not part of the working class. To complicate things, some people who are legally classified as "independent contractors" rather than "employees" are actually wage-workers — for example, couriers (Bickerton and Warskett 2005). Another complication is that there is hierarchy within the working class. For example, many wage-earners report to other workers — supervisors who themselves are employees without substantial management power (for instance, at a university many administrative support staff report to faculty members).[6] This means the working class is more internally divided than is often recognized.

Knowing who belongs to the working class at a particular point in time matters, but it does not tell us all that much. There is tremendous variation in how people who share a common relationship to the system of production and the employing class act and think. This is shaped by many forces that happen over time and across space. These include what employers, governments and other state authorities do; the ups and downs of the capitalist economy; how workers respond to forces they do not control; and how they organize themselves or are organized by others. The way that gender relations, racial practices and ideas, and other dimensions of society are structured shape a working class as it actually exists. Mass media, political parties, religion and other influences on how people make sense of the world may also have an impact.

We can see this clearly if we compare the working class in Canada and Quebec today with the working class in, say, 1919 or 1970.[7] We are still talking about a working class, but the class as it exists today is very different from the class as it existed in either of those two earlier times. It is not just that people's lives in the workplaces where they work for pay, in their households and in their broader communities are different. The subtitle of Thom Workman's 2009 book *If You're In My Way, I'm Walking: The Assault on Working People Since 1970* pinpoints a critical feature of what has been happening over the last several decades. Workman summarizes the assault in this way:

> When compared with the immediate post-war decades [c. 1945-1975] working people have lost considerable ground... more and more working people have endured awful experiences... watched their wages stagnate and sometimes lose ground to inflation, become terribly anxious about the future, been forced into rotten, low-paying jobs and lost all confidence in the country's social programs. The gains that the working class forged in the first half of the twentieth century have been continually rolled back since the 1970s.... These trends will only worsen as the global economy passes through the current economic crisis. (7)

This assault has been part of a major restructuring of society carried out by capitalists, public sector employers, governments and the top ranks of the civil service. This restructuring — sometimes described as neoliberal — has changed how people work and live. These changes have had a big impact on the relations among workers and between the working class and the employing class. I look at these and some other important changes in society in Chapter Six. For now, it is enough to say that the working class has not only been suffering from a decades-long assault, but that changes linked to this assault have undermined (but certainly not eliminated) workers' resistance to employers and governments, eroded unity and solidarity among working-class people and encouraged many workers to buy into the idea that they have to support the measures that employers and governments say are necessary for the sake of Canada's (or Quebec's) economic competitiveness. All this has left its mark on the workers' movement.

The Working-Class Movement

What, then, is the working-class movement? In this book, this term is understood as including all of the organizations through which groups of workers act collectively to defend themselves or improve their conditions of work and life.[8] The largest and best-known components of working-class movements are formal organizations: unions and political parties. There are also other kinds of formal movement organizations, such as community-based groups that take action against racism, sexism or pollution. Working-class movement organization can also be informal. An example of informal organization would be a bunch of people in a non-unionized call centre who work together to persuade their coworkers to all call in sick on a particular day in response to the manager's refusal to deal with their complaints. So working-class movements are made up of a diverse array of formal and informal organizations.

As we will see, the working-class movement in Canada and Quebec today is made up mainly of unions. In this book, people who hold an elected or appointed position in unions are referred to as officials or the officialdom. The officialdom is made up of two groups of people: "officers" (members who are elected or appointed to a position in a union, a minority of whom are "booked off" to perform union work on a full-time paid basis) and "staff" (people who work for unions, who are almost always hired rather than elected from the membership). The term "rank-and-file" refers to the vast majority of union members who hold no official position within the union.

As alluded to in the opening lines of this introduction, some people are skeptical about calling unions today a movement. Some might argue that what New York City subway operator and union activist Steve Downs has said also applies north of the border:

> We speak about the labour movement and I think we tend to do it out of habit or maybe generosity or maybe even embarrassment, but there is no labour movement in this city or in this country, frankly... there is no unifying vision, there are no widely-accepted goals, there certainly is no forward momentum. (2009a)

What Downs says about the lack of vision, goals and momentum in US unions is true. Similar things can be said about unions in Canada and Quebec today. Former long-time union staffer Sid Shniad says simply, "organized labour is not functioning like a movement at all," but as "individual, isolated organizations" (Shniad 2010: 141).

One way of responding to this would be to drop the term working-class (or labour) movement and use another label, like "the mass organizations of the working class." But I prefer to stick with the term working-class movement and to stress that this concept does not imply anything specific about the character of the organizations in question. Working-class movement organizations can be gaining strength and pushing forward (as last happened in Canada and Quebec between the mid-1960s and the mid-1970s [Heron 1996: 85–106]). At exceptional moments, they can pose a radical challenge to the status quo in society (as the Bolivian working-class movement, along with other social movements, did in the early years of the twenty-first century [Webber 2010]). They can also be bureaucratic, divided, in retreat and decaying (as I argue in Chapter Five is the case in Canada and Quebec today).

Does the Movement Matter?

Why bother to read a book about the workers' movement in Canada and Quebec today, or to write one? Isn't the movement an unimportant relic of the early twentieth century, a bit like a dilapidated though once-impressive building that still stands in the downtown of a city whose streets are lined with empty storefronts?

I believe that the working-class movement still matters enormously, despite its very real deficiencies. In Chapter Seven, I make a case that working-class movements are good in ethical terms. To summarize briefly, workers' movements preserve and enhance human life. They can and do allow people to have better access to what they require to meet their needs and to flourish as human beings. This includes higher pay and benefits, shorter hours of work, better workplace health and safety, less management domination on the job, public services that enhance people's health and other progressive changes in society beyond the workplace. But even if we set aside the ethical argument for now, there are still two reasons why the workers' movement today is important.

First, quite simply, the only organizations that workers can use to defend themselves in a society in which they are under assault are their own independent organizations. Unions and other working-class movement organizations today are far from ideal, but they are all that workers have to defend themselves, improve working and living conditions or try to change society in larger ways. The courts have been of little use to workers, since the law generally defends the power of the employing class (Panitch and Swartz 2003; Fudge 2008; Fine 1984). For example, fired workers who go to court claiming unjust dismissal and win almost never get their jobs back. None of the major political parties consistently defends the working class. The NDP, the party traditionally backed by many unions, has never opposed the neoliberal reorganization of capitalism that has inflicted so much harm on workers over the last three decades (see Chapter Six). Academics, journalists and community leaders supportive of social justice can analyze or speak out against the assault on workers, but perceptive analysis and fine words by themselves have little or no impact on what employers and governments actually do. Workers cannot rely on anyone but themselves, using the existing organizations of the workers' movement, changing them and creating new ones.

The other reason working-class movements matter is that it is through movement organizations that working people can develop their capacities to think and act for social change. Analyzing what is happening in the workplace and beyond and organizing collective action to make progressive change are skills that must be learned. What is taught in schools, colleges and universities — and how it is taught — rarely helps workers to become independent thinkers who can analyze the problems they face in society in ways that are rooted in their needs and experiences. How to organize collective action against injustice is never on the curriculum. Workers' capacities to think and act in their own interests must be nurtured elsewhere in the movement[9] (how much of this is actually happening in the movement today is another issue that will be discussed).

Unfortunately, the working-class movement in Canada and Quebec today is in crisis, as I show in Part One of this book. Its condition is certainly not as dire as that of its counterpart in the U.S.[10] Nevertheless, it is divided and retreating. Worse, it is changing in ways that add up to a process of decay. Unions are still institutions that regulate employer-employee relations for a large minority of wage earners. But it is becoming somewhat harder for workers to use unions as organizations to resist demands that they give up past gains. Most of the union officialdom is putting up little resistance to these demands for concessions. Democracy within unions is suffering. Unions are becoming more distant from non-unionized workers, as the union presence in the private sector where most people work for wages is now very weak, and people of colour, who are a growing proportion of the working class, are under-represented among unionized workers. Older members dominate many unions and there are fewer young union activists, which distances unions from younger members and youth in general. Political action by unions is increasingly about backing parties and candidates who, rhetoric aside, do not oppose the assault on workers. Unions are becoming less effective for unionized workers and less significant for the working class as a whole. All this means that workers are less likely to see unions as organizations through which they can act together in their own interests. As a result, they are less likely to reclaim unions as working-class movement organizations.

Faced with this situation, what is called for is not just an attempt to energize the movement in its current form but efforts to make sweeping changes that would reinvent the movement. The working-class movement has been remade in the past to respond to how capitalism changed, and it could be reinvented again as a more effective vehicle for the struggles of working people. This would be a long process, and there are many barriers to transforming the movement, but it is necessary to try. The focus of Part Two is why the movement should be reinvented and why people should try to reinvent it by reforming unions from below and building new workers' organizations, rather than by taking a reform from above approach.

About This Book

This book is written both for students and other readers whose main interest is simply to understand the subject better and for people who are involved in a union or other activist organization and want to contribute to reviving the movement. It is organized into two Parts. Part One opens with three chapters that examine different dimensions of unions, followed by a brief look at other organizations. The fifth chapter offers an overall assessment of the movement as it currently exists. The sixth chapter explains how it has come to be the way it is. Part Two looks forward, asking the question "why reinvent the movement?" and then considering different approaches to trying to change and strengthen it.

To understand the working-class movement as it exists in Canada and Quebec today, it is more important to examine what people actually *do* through its organizations than what is written in policy documents or what top leaders say in speeches. This emphasis is reflected in this book. Because unions are by far the largest working-class movement organizations, with tens of thousands of active members, most of this book is about unions. Throughout, the focus is on unions at the levels at which most workers encounter them, not on the goings-on among top officers and staff.

Readers who are not familiar with the initials of the names of unions and other organizations can consult the list of acronyms provided. There is also a brief Concepts section where key terms used in the book are defined (most of them are also explained when they first appear in the text). The Resources and Readings section offers suggestions for people who want to deepen their understanding of issues discussed in the book and for people who are (or want to become) activists and are looking for useful resources.

My assessment of unions today is often very critical. This may lead some readers to accuse me of not respecting the many thousands of people whose often thankless efforts keep unions going. In fact, the exact opposite is the case. It is precisely because I respect their hard work and commitment that I believe union activists deserve a serious examination of the movement as it is today, warts and all, and how to try to change it. This is what I have tried to offer readers.

Notes

1. <canadianlabour.ca>

2. In this book, I use "Canada" to refer to what some call "English Canada" or "the rest of Canada" — in other words, the provinces other than Quebec. Quebec is a nation within a multinational state made up of Canada, Quebec and indigenous nations. To avoid ignoring Quebec's distinct national reality, which is reflected in how the Quebec workers' movement is organized, I do not include it when referring to "Canada." I use the term "indigenous" rather than "aboriginal" following the argument in Alfred 2005 (126–32).

3. My discussion of class and the working-class movement draws on Camfield 2008. For the class theory that underpins how class is understood in this book, see Meiksins 1986 and Camfield 2004/2005; Meiksins 1986 and 1989 offer critiques of some other influential approaches to class theory.

4. In theoretical terms, they are all part of the collective labourer, to use a term of Karl Marx's. "Privileged, skilled, autonomous workers are still wage-labourers, whose privileges, skills and autonomy are under constant threat of removal by capitalists" (Meiksins 1986: 112). That said, managerial employees in positions from which there is "a real possibility of promotion into upper management — with the virtual ending of exposure to deskilling, unemployment and the like" are in "ambiguous class positions" rather than being part of the working class (113).

5. Just to give one example, higher-paid workers with "professional" status often identify more with the managers they work under than with the clerical workers they work with or the people who clean the buildings in which they work. As a result, they often do not support the struggles of such groups of lower-status, lower-paid workers.

6. This fact does not prove that employees with authority over others, even a lot of authority, are not part of the working class. There is a long history of hierarchical authority relations among workers on the job. For example, in the 1800s, skilled craftspeople like molders and coopers "often hired and fired their own helpers and paid the latter some fixed portion of their own earnings" (Montgomery 1979: 11). Today, for example, some university faculty hire and pay research assistants. Craft workers were a high-paid, high-status section of the working class then (and generally had elitist attitudes to match); the same can be said today about regular university faculty (precariously employed contract faculty have much lower pay and status).

7. The best introduction to the history of the working class in Canada and Quebec is still Palmer 1992.

8. In more theoretical terms, organizations through which workers resist class exploitation (on which see Lebowitz 2006), alienation (Rinehart 2006: 11–18), oppression (such as sexism, racism and heterosexism) and other forms of harm. In Canada and Quebec today, active members of working-class movement organizations rarely see these organizations as such. This matters, but does not mean they are not objectively part of a working-class movement.

9. There are some interesting thoughts on working-class capacities in Gindin 1998a (especially 76–83); subsequent developments (discussed in Chapter Eight) raise questions about the account of the CAW in the late 1990s presented there. On schooling today (whose methods sometimes still influence union education) see Sears 2003, which from 246–57 discusses an alternative approach of "education for freedom."

10. On unions in the U.S. today, see Moody 2007 and Early 2011.

Part One

The Working-Class Movement Today

1. Unions and the Workplace[1]

One day in the late 1990s, the majority of nurses and doctors in the Emergency Department at Vancouver General Hospital walked into the office of the CEO and refused to leave unless the much-loved unit manager, a "tireless advocate for her staff, and the department's patients" who had been fired without cause, was rehired. They won their demand.[2] Action of this kind by unionized workers was once not uncommon, but is now extremely rare. Unionism as it exists today is based on contracts, not direct action.

For most people in Canada and Quebec who have first-hand experience with unions, what they have encountered is connected to provisions in a collective agreement (contract) negotiated between a union and an employer (or in some cases more than one union and one or more than one employer). Bargaining for a collective agreement and attempting to ensure that employers abide by the rights and procedures contained in it are the central activities of unions. Linked to that is the effort to encourage workers to insist on their rights, since "a lot of people don't want to cause waves in the workplace so they don't enforce the collective agreement."[3] Other activities, such as member education and mobilization, are generally geared to contract bargaining and enforcement. Contracts are often long documents written using technical language that is difficult for most people to interpret. As a result, most union members turn to a union officer or staff person when they have questions about their rights and obligations under the contract.

Unionism in Canada has not always revolved around the collective agreement in this way; contract unionism was the result of historic changes in labour law and the nature of unions that took place in the 1940s, which will be discussed in Chapter Six. Prior to these changes, written contracts were short or non-existent. Shop stewards — shop floor workers elected to represent their fellow union members in dealings with management and who often organized work stoppages and other forms of direct action when conflicts arose — were often central in enforcing workers' rights. What one Chrysler worker activist in the U.S. said in the mid-1950s with only slight exaggeration was equally true in Canada: "'In the old days, he [the steward] was the Union, he was the Contract'" (Lichtenstein 2002: 125). This do-it-yourself direct action unionism, prohibited by law since the mid-1940s, has almost entirely disappeared. It is not even a memory for most union members today.

In its place, what has trade unionism become? For many unionized workers, "the union" means someone outside their immediate workplace — a steward (sometimes called a representative or some other title), member of their local's executive board or staff representative (often called a business agent) — whom they can contact when they have questions or concerns about their collective agreement rights. Workers in some especially conservative and undemocratic unions whose officials show no interest in members most of the time may have difficulty even contacting an official. But often the face of the union is a coworker who is a steward. However, in many union locals today, it is common to find some steward positions vacant because no one in certain units or departments is willing to stand for election (or appointment) or because the local's executive has not tried to fill the vacancies. A few unions have moved away from making stewards the front line of defence for workers' rights in the workplace, or never had a system of stewards to begin with. In such unions, workers with concerns are usually directed to phone an office or call centre rather than to speak with a steward. For example, members of the Nova Scotia Government and General Employees Union are asked to call the union's Labour Resource Centre (LRC). Staff at the LRC turn grievances over to other staff — Employee Relations Officers.[4] In a variation on the theme of "professionalizing" the union's front-line presence, the B.C. Nurses' Union (BCNU) has created full-time paid stewards who are hired, not elected. This has reduced the role of volunteers who continue to serve as stewards while working as nurses.[5]

When workers turn to "the union," they usually do so for representation — for someone serving as an official representative of the union to act on their behalf. Workers often expect that union officials will take care of their problems for them. A former Canadian Auto Workers (CAW) staff representative describes this common pattern: "People call up as if I'm a lawyer on retainer, and say 'Here's my problem, solve it for me, and phone me when it's done.'" Although she observes, "I don't think that benefits the working class at all to have that kind of a relationship" and "the more people who do it themselves, in conjunction with their fellow workers... the stronger and better I think it is,"[6] it is not common for union officials to urge workers to take a more active role in addressing their workplace problems.

When it is thought that management has violated a right enshrined in the collective agreement, the only response allowed under labour law is to file a grievance (unionists sometimes turn to health and safety law or human rights legislation if the contract offers no recourse). The contract is the touchstone of workers' rights, since anything not covered in its provisions cannot be grieved. "Obey now, grieve later" has long been the rule of workplace unionism. Strikes during a collective agreement — "wildcats" — are illegal. The scope of what can be grieved is restricted not only to matters that are covered by provisions of the collective agreement, but also by the management's rights clauses found in contracts. These give formal blessing to the right of employers to run enterprises and workplaces unilaterally in every respect except where the contract specifically limits their authority. In these ways, the ability of union activists to defend workers in the workplace is severely limited (Rinehart 2006: 202–204).

Once filed, a grievance — an allegation that the employer has violated the contract — enters a dispute resolution procedure that can be lengthy. Decisions about the handling of the grievance are made by union officials rather than by the worker or workers affected. The pursuit of grievances, especially when they proceed to arbitration, demands an attention to evidence, wording, past practices and prior rulings by arbitrators that makes it similar in many ways to a court hearing. This influences what skills union activists learn through experience and what is taught in union education programs. U.S. labour lawyer Thomas Geoghegan's remark that "The entire labor movement is like a giant bar association of non-licensed attorneys" (in Lichtenstein 2002: 125) is an exaggeration, but it does capture an important dimension of unions in Canada and Quebec today.

Another dimension of unionism organized around the defence of collective agreements is less noticed, but equally important for workers: the union as a defender of management's authority. Contracts are double-edged swords. In addition to placing at least some restraints on what employers can do, they also ratify employer authority in the workplace. Union officials are legally required to uphold contracts, ensuring workers comply with their rules. Some employers have become quite successful at enlisting union officials into the running of their operations. This is especially true in unionized private sector firms where union leaders have been persuaded or intimidated into cooperating with employers in order to boost the competitiveness of the company in the belief this will save jobs. A veteran activist in the CAW describes the situation in auto assembly plants in this way:

> Locally managements have responded by consciously taking advantage of this weakening of the union's power on the shop floor due to both this ongoing weakening of our local agreements and to workers' pervasive fear of job losses by shrewdly and meticulously integrating shop floor union leaderships into the process of managing operations without compromising management's agenda. Increasingly rank-and-file workers have found it harder to tell the difference between the message they hear from in-plant union leaderships and what they hear from the boss. (Allen 2009a: 14)

A similar situation in private sector unions in Quebec is described by long-time observer Jean-Marc Piotte, who argues that many unions have accepted employer schemes for the organization of work that suppress "the space

for dispute, and therefore unionism, within the very organization of work"
(2008: 103; my translation). It should not come as a surprise, then, that some
unionized workers do not experience the union as protecting them from
management's power.

In recent decades, the union whose members were most likely to try to
deal with workplace problems by means other than those stipulated by law
and collective agreement was the Canadian Union of Postal Workers (CUPW).
However, employer efforts at Canada Post have brought CUPW into line. As a
CUPW activist with over three decades of experience as a workplace activist
and union official put it in 2008:

> Ten years ago in a lot of the sections in Canada Post, in a lot of
> the sections and facilities in the major plants [t]here was very much
> control on the workfloor, directing the locals, and directing the region
> [CUPW regional office], on how things are going to be done — walk-
> outs, sitdowns, all of that kind of thing. Whereas now, that's not the
> situation. Now the grievance procedure basically is what everyone
> talks about in terms of solving their problems.

Union reliance on the grievance procedure has significant effects:

> The grievance procedure... doesn't empower workers on the
> workfloor. It doesn't empower workers to say to the boss "I'm not
> doing that"... because the boss'll say "well, do it now and grieve
> later"... to take that away... really does take away the first level of
> power in a union... in most cases, it [the grievance procedure]...
> doesn't build a militant union in a workplace... and it doesn't build
> a participatory union because people start relying on the grievance
> procedure to solve their problems for them, rather than saying the
> group of workers in that section have to solve their problems for
> themselves. And that's the only way a union can really build itself,
> and that's the way the CUPW used to do things.

The reliance on the grievance procedure is not the only way that the approach
to workplace problems in CUPW has changed. Union officers no longer try to
actively involve workers in responding to issues in the workplace:

> The way the union reacts now to consultations... is that... the local
> leadership of the union goes in and does those consultations. At one
> time it used to be common to bring people from the workfloor into
> those consultations, so that they could basically tell management
> why it won't work, why the schedule changes, perhaps, won't
> work.... Now I'm finding that... local leadership everywhere takes
> over that.[7]

With these changes, CUPW now generally conforms with the reliance on the grievance and arbitration system that has been standard in Canadian unions since the middle of the twentieth century.

Incidents of workplace direct action like the one mentioned at the beginning of this chapter do still occasionally happen, although they are rarely reported. But for decades, this kind of direct action has been extremely rare. Wildcat strikes, some of which happen when workers stop work to respond to a workplace issue, have almost disappeared in recent years. On construction sites, where job action was once, in the words of a veteran unionist, "a viable tool," the threat of employers responding by bringing in non-union contractors to do the work has led to such stoppages becoming much less common.[8] In 2008, as the economic crisis hit hard, there were only two strikes during a collective agreement reported, the fewest ever.[9] Unionism that accepts the channeling of workplace disputes into grievance and arbitration hearings by law and contract is the norm.

Who Is Covered?

About three in ten wage-earners are covered by a union collective agreement. The union density rate — the percentage of people in paid employment outside of agriculture who are in unions — has been slowly falling from its peak of 41.8 percent in 1984. The main causes of this overall decline have been the faster growth of employment in non-unionized firms than in already-unionized operations and the slow pace of non-unionized workers organizing into unions. By 1997, union density had reached 33.7 percent (Jackson and Schetagne 2004: 63–64). In 2009, it was 29.5 percent. The Statistics Canada data on union density is not an exact measurement of the percentage of wage-earning members of the working class who belong to unions, but serves as a close approximation.[10] More importantly, there is a huge difference between the rates of unionization in the private and public sectors: 16.1 percent and 71.3 percent in 2009. This is connected to the difference in union density along gender lines: 30.8 percent for women, who are more likely to work for state agencies or state-funded organizations, and 28.2 percent among men (Statistics Canada 2009: 27).

Who is outside the scope of unions' collective agreement protection? Simply from the point of view of numbers, more significant than the legal denial of the right to unionize to some groups is the very low unionization rate among the majority of wage-earners who are employed by for-profit firms. It is noteworthy that some groups of workers, such as agricultural and domestic workers — both largely people of colour admitted into Canada as temporary migrant workers and subjected to intensely racist and, for women, sexist working and living conditions (Choudry et al. 2009) — remain barred from collective bargaining by law in some provinces (ITUC 2007). The 2007

Supreme Court of Canada's ruling in the *Health Services* case that extends limited protection under the Charter of Rights and Freedoms to collective bargaining may eventually lead to the elimination of many of these blatant exclusions (Fudge 2008).

Another gap runs along the social division caused by racism. People of colour are less likely to be unionized than white workers. People of colour make up more than 16 percent of the population, a dramatic shift from the 4.7 percent reported in 1981 (Statistics Canada 2008b). The rate of unionization among workers of colour is just over 20 percent, about a third lower than the overall rate.[11] This is not because workers of colour are less pro-union than white workers — if anything, the opposite is true. Instead, it is the result of systemic racism that streams people of colour into poorly paid, low-status and non-union jobs at a higher rate than whites (Galabuzi 2006: 98). This low unionization rate may well become even more pronounced if, as predicted, current immigration trends lead to people of colour reaching one-fifth of the population by 2017 (Statistics Canada 2008b) and if the dynamics of unionization and employment among workers of colour remain unchanged. Factoring in the rapidly growing indigenous population (3.8 percent of the population was defined by the 2006 census as Aboriginal [Statistics Canada 2008a]) only underscores how many working-class people face racial oppression. But the unionized working class is disproportionately white; workers of colour are less likely to fall under the umbrella of a collective agreement than white workers. How this affects unions when it comes to responding to racism in the working class and society more broadly will be discussed later. Now, having examined how contracts are the backbone of unions as they exist today, let us turn to what is happening when unions go to the negotiating table.

Collective Bargaining Today

The secure legal rights to form a union and bargain collectively over a range of economic issues — pay, benefits, hours of work, vacations and workplace rights — were the chief gains that unionized workers accepted in the 1940s in exchange for tight restrictions on when and over what issues they could strike (Fudge and Tucker 2001: 263–15). In the 1960s, public sector workers fought to extend these rights beyond the private sector and municipal government where they had been established during and shortly after the Second World War; they were eventually successful in gaining the right to unionize and bargain in almost every case, but some were denied the right to strike.

Beginning in the mid-1970s, free collective bargaining has been violated more than one hundred times by federal and provincial governments passing legislation to impose pay caps, dictate other contract terms, suspend the right to strike or force a strike to end (Panitch and Swartz 2003; Fudge 2006). The workers affected have usually been in the broader public sector (governments and state-funded organizations, including health-care facilities, schools, colleges, universities and social service agencies). Since "the *effective* right to bargain collectively requires the ability of workers in concert to withdraw their labour — the 'right to strike'" (Fudge 2006: 8; emphasis added), these state actions have substantially undermined collective bargaining for the majority of union members who work in the public sector. For their part, unionized private sector workers find themselves dealing with employers in the context of the most unfavourable balance of power in bargaining since the Great Depression of the 1930s, due to how business and government have restructured capitalism over the last three decades (see Chapter Six).

Unions today bargain collectively on behalf of their members and their members only. Labour law dictates that unions represent only employees covered by their collective agreements; they cannot act on behalf of the working class more broadly. Almost all gains by unions for non-unionized workers are indirect: some non-union employers peg their wages to those at unionized competitors. In addition, collective bargaining is highly fragmented: the bargaining unit, the legally-defined group of workers covered by a particular contract, is generally defined quite narrowly. For example, on a university campus, the unionized workforce sharing the same employer will usually be divided into separate bargaining units of faculty, contract teaching staff, teaching assistants, academic support staff and non-academic support staff. Each of these will usually bargain on its own and most will belong to different union locals. Contracts covering workers across an industry in the private sector have become uncommon, since many corporate employers have been successful in their efforts over the past three decades to break out of broader bargaining arrangements in favour of dealing with workers in different places and firms separately. The result of this state-fashioned system of negotiations is that the bargaining efforts of each of the many segments of the unionized section of the working class are confined to their own immediate concerns and rarely united even with one other small segment, thereby weakening workers' power in negotiations. The range of concerns over which bargaining takes place is also limited; management's rights clauses and union custom rule out all but very minor challenges to how employers run their organizations and workplaces.

In most unions, the mass of workers themselves have little control over bargaining, the central activity of the organization. In unions that are relatively more democratic, bargaining proposals are brought to membership meetings for adoption and bargaining teams made up of members are elected and report back to the membership from time to time. In some unions, though, the bargaining team is appointed by the elected executive, not elected directly by members. Even where teams are elected, decisions about what demands will be taken to the negotiating table are often made with only a little member input, such as a survey of members' priorities, or none at all. Once underway, it is very rare for members to be able to exert much influence over how their bargainers handle negotiations. Union staff rather than members often play the leading role at the table.

There are exceptions to these standard approaches, such as the innovative way CUPE Local 3903 handled bargaining during its eleven-week strike against York University in 2000–2001:

> Our bargaining practices gradually coalesced around a model that discouraged the bargaining team (and Executive) from constituting themselves as disconnected entities separate from, and unaccountable to, the membership.... This model conceived the bargaining team as accountable and responsive to an active (rather than passive) membership, taking direction from the membership on an ongoing basis. (Kuhling 2002: 78)

However, this level of openness and democratic accountability is extremely unusual. Efforts to mobilize members in support of bargainers at the table, in order to apply pressure on the employer, are more common than experiments in making the process of collective bargaining more democratic.

To make matters worse, too often union officials end up bargaining alone, without much support from members of other locals of the same union, other unions, community groups or anyone else. Yet mobilization and solidarity-building initiatives have become increasingly necessary as unions find themselves forced to contend with a deteriorating balance of power in bargaining. Collective bargaining in recent years "has often entailed extensive efforts to overhaul union agreements to give management increased flexibility in employment, deployment, and wages" (Albo and Crow 2005). The erosion or elimination of pensions and other benefits also needs to be added to this list of employer goals. So, too, are measures that draw unions closer to employers and reduce their ability to act as independent organizations that champion workers' interests.

Unionized workers do enjoy higher wages than non-unionized workers doing comparable work. In the 1990s, the union wage premium — how much higher the wages of unionized workers are compared to the wages of non-unionized workers — was between 7 and 14 percent. The premium is highest for workers who otherwise would be lower-paid, including young workers, workers of colour, women workers and workers with fewer years of schooling (Jackson 2005: 152–53). But signs of how the balance of bargaining power has been tilting still further in the direction of employers are clear to see.

One is the increasing length of contracts. Agreements signed in 2005 averaged 47.1 months in length, 42.6 months in 2006, 37 months in 2007 and 41.6 months in 2008.[12] Although in some circumstances a strong union may prefer a longer contract in order to lock-in gains for an extended period of time, such contracts mean that unionized workers have to wait longer for their next opportunity to use the threat of withdrawing their labour power to try to improve wages, benefits and working conditions. A longer lull between rounds of bargaining generally weakens a union. Because collective bargaining is the central activity of unions most of the time, and the one usually most likely to motivate members to get involved in some kind of union activity, a union usually becomes more inactive when more years pass between rounds of collective bargaining. Employers are well aware of this, and often prefer longer contracts so they less often have to face the possibility of workers going on strike. On the other hand, workers confident in their collective power and ability to use it are likely to prefer shorter contracts and more frequent opportunities to bargain for gains. The trend since the closing years of the twentieth century towards longer contracts is the opposite of this. Fearful of future demands for deeper concessions and doubtful of their ability to resist, many union officials have been ready to negotiate longer deals and workers have usually been willing to ratify them so as to have more years until the next ordeal.

In spite of the employers' offensive that has been underway since the mid-1970s (see Chapter Six), some groups of unionized workers have still been able to win small victories. Unions whose members are in high demand in the job market have had the fewest difficulties. For example, in 2008, unionized nurses in Saskatchewan ratified a four-year deal that raises the pay of general-duty nurses by more than one-third (Conway 2009). But even workers who do not have the advantage of being in an occupation in short supply have been able to make some gains through determined action. Coordinated bargaining and mobilization among workers at some forty hotels in Quebec in 2008, involving both short walk-outs and some longer strikes, succeeded in winning gains for a mostly female and often women-of-colour workforce. These included one fewer room to clean per shift for housekeepers during summer months and on weekends and a reduction in the use of staff from temp agencies (Piotte 2009). Such improvements in a time of capitalist crisis and aggressive employers' offensive are not easily achieved. Nevertheless, contrary to what many people believe, they are not impossible, even for low-paid private sector workers if workers are able to mobilize effectively.

However, concessionary bargaining is today much more common than negotiating improvements. Most private and public sector employers come to the table with demands that unions give up existing benefits and rights and accept wage cuts, freezes or increases below the rate of inflation. Proposals that draw unions into close collaboration with employers to achieve employer goals at the expense of workers' interests are also frequently tabled. Employers are usually able to achieve much of what they seek, including the elimination of jobs. In the words of former senior CAW staffer Sam Gindin, "It used to be that corporations promised jobs [in exchange] for concessions; now they aggressively demand more concessions alongside *fewer* jobs" (Gindin 2009a).

The 2008 contracts negotiated between the CAW and the "Detroit Three" motor vehicle firms (General Motors, Chrysler and Ford) and the reopening of these contracts in 2009 illustrate the state of collective bargaining. These negotiations were widely reported and discussed. They involved huge multinational corporations hit hard by the economic crisis and a union that in the 1980s and 1990s had won gains for auto assembly workers that made their wages and benefits the envy of many other workers. In 208, in a move Gindin noted "had an air of panic about it" (2008), CAW officials made the surprise move of going into bargaining early. They emerged with three-year deals that contained a lump-sum payment instead of an increase to base pay, no cost-of-living allowances, one week less vacation time and weaker prescription drug coverage. New hires would be paid 70 percent of the base rate rather than 85 percent and would take three years to reach the base, with weaker benefits and less vacation time (Gindin 2008). In 2009, CAW officials reopened these agreements and gave wage and benefit concessions valued at some seven dollars per hour for GM workers, with the contract extended by another year. Still more concessions followed for workers at Chrysler, prompting even deeper give-backs at GM. The Chrysler-GM "pattern" was then matched at Ford. Little-noticed by outside observers, the path to these dramatic give-backs without a fight had been paved by years of concessionary local agreements negotiated at each assembly plant in addition to the company-wide master agreements (Allen 2009a). In 2008 and 2009, as CAW officials sold downward spiralling concessions to members as necessary in order to meet government conditions for loan guarantees for GM and Chrysler, auto workers received little sympathy from other workers. "Anger and frustration of other workers against the CAW's appeals for the auto loan guarantees reflect[ed] the union's distance from the working class as a whole" (Rosenfeld 2009: 31b).

The CAW is far from the only union to give concessions without a struggle. For example, the officialdom of the United Food and Commercial Workers (UFCW) has become well-known for putting up only token resistance to demands for concessions.[13] Since the mid-1980s, grocery retail workers have experienced UFCW officials agreeing to contracts with "wage reductions, two-tiered and multi-tiered wage structures, downsizing of the full-time workforce and the expansion of low-paid part-time workers" (Kainer 2002: 155). These concessions have fallen particularly hard on women, who make up most of the part-time grocery retail workforce and most of the service (as opposed to production) jobs in the industry (166–84). Concessions bargaining is certainly not limited to the private sector. The high-profile 2009 Toronto municipal workers' strike, discussed below, is but one example.

A union agreeing to accept less than it had before negotiations began is not the only way collective bargaining can produce a weaker union. Members of the CUPW, a union born out of a wildcat strike in 1965 by postal workers with no union rights (Ostroff 1996) that still has a reputation for militancy and left-wing politics, found themselves embroiled in debate during the union's 2007 negotiations for its main urban bargaining unit. The tentative agreement recommended by eight of the fifteen members of CUPW's National Executive Board (NEB) and opposed by the other seven contained a Corporate Team Incentive (CTI) proposed by Canada Post. CTI pays all workers a bonus if Canada Post decides that its corporate objectives have been met. This added compensation at the discretion of the employer to the contract. It also acts as a carrot to entice workers to strive to meet the goals of the employer, even though the employer alone decides if Canada Post's objectives have been met and a bonus will be paid. In this way, CTI serves as a tool to weaken the union. Yet the majority of the NEB recommended the agreement containing CTI without even holding a strike authorization vote to mobilize members and back up negotiators at the bargaining table (Mooney 2007).[14]

Overall, collective bargaining is not working for workers. As a former CAW staffer put it, "It's not working. The way we do things... gets them more than the non-unionized workers, but it isn't really making any advances for workers."[15]

Striking in Hard Times

So far this examination of unions and bargaining has focused on negotiations that do not involve strikes or lockouts. As the balance of forces between the dominant class and the working class has become worse for workers, strikes have become less and less common. Almost all of the strikes that have taken place in recent years have been defensive efforts to fend off concessions rather than attempts to improve workers' pay or working conditions. During the 1980s, when the employers' offensive that began in the mid-1970s picked up steam, the number of workers on strike or locked out per year averaged 365,900. The 1990s saw that number fall to 178,700.[16] The trend since the turn of the century has been one of further decline, with a sharp drop-off beginning two years before the global economic crisis hit Canada and Quebec in 2008:

2000	142,672
2001	221,145

2002	165,590
2003	78,765
2004	259,229
2005	199,007
2006	42,314
2007	65,552
2008	41,308
2009	67,193[17]

As Thom Workman argues, the decline in workers' willingness to strike is the result of the "climate of neoliberal austerity deliberately forged by governments and materially cemented by decades of intensified corporate restructuring." This has made most workers fearful "and weakened the overall resistance of the labour movement" (Workman 2009: 66, 67).

Strike outcomes have become less positive for workers. Many strikes end in defeat. In part, this can be explained by forces that are beyond the control of even the most dynamic and mobilized single union, as we will see in Chapter Six. But in many cases, union weaknesses also contribute to defeats.

The 2005 strike of the Telecommunications Workers Union (TWU) against Telus in British Columbia and Alberta illustrates the kinds of problems many private sector unions face when they withdraw their labour-power. The telecommunications industry has undergone extensive restructuring since the 1980s. Changes have included the establishment of non-unionized subsidiary firms, the introduction of new technologies and massive job losses. This restructuring has "vastly increase[d] the power of telecommunications companies, relative to that of their unionized employees" (Shniad 2007: 300). TWU was forced to strike after trying for no fewer than five years to bargain a new contract covering both the members in B.C. who were formerly employees of B.C. Tel and the members gained in Alberta after Telus and B.C. Tel merged in 1999. At the heart of the dispute was the employer's determination to eliminate two key rights B.C. Tel workers enjoyed: protection against contracting out and the inclusion of technicians in the bargaining unit. But as a TWU staffer wrote:

> Little or no effort was made — either by the TWU or the wider labour movement — to generate a plan of action capable of forcing Telus to back off. As a result, organized labour's actions proved inadequate in the face of Telus' comprehensive strategy, which in-

cluded the hiring of thousands of scabs imported from central and eastern Canada and the United States.... In addition, Telus made unprecedented use of "security" companies whose employees made picketers' lives miserable by engaging in picket line harassment and intimidation. (305)

Telus succeeded in dividing members in Alberta, more than half of whom were scabbing by the time the strike ended, from workers in B.C. The settlement reached saw the TWU lose the key protections it had won at B.C. Tel. The aftershocks of the defeat included bitter infighting among top TWU officers and their supporters (306-308).

Both the potential power and real weaknesses of contemporary unions were exposed in a dramatic strike in B.C. the year before TWU's ordeal. Some 8,000 members of the Hospital Employees Union (HEU), many of them women of colour, lost their jobs to contracting-out after the provincial Liberal government passed Bill 29 in 2002. This law enabled the privatization, elimination or transfer of health services. It also stripped the strong no-contracting-out language, successor rights (which transfer workers' collective agreements to their new employers when privatization or contracting-out happens) and other rights out of the contract that covers B.C. health support workers. Regaining protection against contracting-out was a central goal of HEU's 2004 strike. The strike received strong support from working people across B.C. As expected, the provincial government quickly passed back-to-work legislation. What was unexpected was how harsh the legislation was. Instead of sending the unresolved issues to an arbitrator to settle, Bill 37 imposed a contract that cut wages 11 percent retroactively, increased the length of the work week with no increase in pay (amounting to another 4 percent pay cut) and provided no protection against contracting-out. HEU's leadership decided to defy the legislation and continue the strike. Other unionized workers began to demand action to support HEU. A few groups of workers went further and struck in solidarity, triggering a day of strikes by some 18,000 CUPE members and smaller numbers of other public and private sector workers. Labour and community activists prepared to escalate solidarity actions to help HEU beat back Bill 37. Meanwhile, top leaders of the B.C. Federation of Labour put pressure on HEU's top officials to end the strike. A week after the strike began, a deal was reached that slightly softened the blow of Bill 37: wage cuts would not be retroactive, job losses as a direct result of contracting out were limited to the equivalent of 600 full-time positions over two years, and $25 million in severance funds would be provided. HEU's provincial executive voted to end the strike; HEU members were not allowed to vote on the deal. It was a demoralizing defeat not only for the strikers who had walked the lines with courage and determination, but for the many workers who had seen the strike as a chance to deal a blow to a hated right-wing government (Camfield 2006).

While not all strikes have gone as badly for workers as these two struggles in western provinces did, for many years there have been rather more strikes ending in defeat for workers than victory. In some cases, though, strikes have been able to at least prevent employers from extracting as many concessions as they had hoped. A close look at the 2009 strike by City of Toronto workers reveals much about the state of the working-class movement today.

Setback in a Key Strike: Toronto Municipal Workers 2009

In the summer of 2009, more than 24,000 Toronto municipal government employees, members of CUPE Locals 79 and 416, found themselves on the picket lines from June 22 to July 29. This was an important strike. It involved the largest union (CUPE) and its largest local (Local 79) in the largest city in the land. Much as the CAW's high-profile 2009 deals with GM, Chrysler and Ford helped set the tone for how private-sector unions would respond to employer demands for concessions during the economic crisis, the City of Toronto strike sent the signal to workers and employers that public sector workers would be made to suffer, too. Faced with a thick package of demands for concessions and an employer prepared to force a strike to extract them, the leaderships of both of Toronto's municipal workers' locals called members out to defend their contracts. The size and location of the strike made it more prominent than the 101-day strike of Windsor's municipal workforce, which lasted from April 15 until July 24, when it ended with a settlement that saw current workers agree to give up post-retirement benefits for future hires (CBCnews.ca 2009a). In Toronto, most concessions were fended off but the leaders of Locals 79 and 416 signed contracts that gave the employer some of the changes to sick-leave provisions it wanted by giving up the existing plan for all future hires. Worse, the way the strike played out was a setback for the working-class movement (Barnett and Fanelli 2009).

In the only joint strike bulletin issued to members during the thirty-eight day strike, the two local presidents wrote, "When we entered collective bargaining early this year, we did not imagine that you would be walking picket lines by summer" (Dembinski and Ferguson 2009). Unfortunately, this attitude persisted right up until the walkout began. As one strike organizer in CUPE 79 put it six days into the strike:

> It's nothing short of chaos. Our leadership refused to mobilize and organize for a possible strike due to the position they held [that] "we're settling with the employer." I cannot begin to even explain what kind of disastrous situation we're in as a result of such [a] lack of organizing pre-strike.[18]

Local leaders did not clearly explain to members the issues on which they were refusing to give concessions before the strike started.[19] The failure to prepare for the strike resulted in an almost complete absence of communication between the locals' leaders and striking workers once it began. Dedicated members worked hard to keep the strike running at the most basic level, but picketers usually had no leaflets explaining what the strike was about to hand out to passers-by. Very few bulletins were produced for members of either or both locals. No membership meetings of any kind were held. This left strikers feeling isolated and in the dark (Barnett and Fanelli 2009: 27).

Television, radio, newspapers and websites were, predictably, filled with hostile coverage of the strike. The unions were portrayed as greedy and unrealistic for trying to defend paid sick day provisions in their contracts that were better than those of most workers. The fact that these provisions had been agreed to by their employer in exchange for monetary concessions by the unions in the past was almost never mentioned in the media.[20] There was much media hype about the inconveniences caused by the lack of municipal services, including garbage collection and child care centres. All this contributed to what columnist Thomas Walkom described as the "unusual... visceral level of hostility against the strikers that emerges in casual conversation: The workers are uppity; they are already paid too much; they should all be fired" (Walkom 2009).

In the face of this barrage, the top officers of CUPE 79 and 416 provided extremely poor leadership. They did very little to rally members' resolve and counter the wave of hostile accusations. They did even less to make a case for why the defence of decent public sector jobs at the City of Toronto during an economic crisis was in the interest of all working people in the largest city in the country, particularly women and workers of colour (a clear majority of the strikers were women and/or people of colour). As columnist Rick Salutin wrote, "There's an excuse-me quality to the Toronto civic employees' strike. 'We knew it was not going to be a popular strike,' said union leader Ann Dembinski [president of Local 79]. She didn't request support, just 'for the public to be understanding'" (Salutin 2009). It fell to writer Linda McQuaig to make the public case that the unions were "holding the line against employers taking advantage of the recession to demand concessions (if unions simply give in, emboldened employers will go for more), and taking a stand against further erosion of public services" (McQuaig 2009). The lack of effort to fight for the hearts and minds of strikers and other people in the region was clear to see on the websites of both locals, key resources for anyone interested in the unions' side of the story (and for members of the locals). Strikers were never brought together in large marches, rallies or other mass actions that could have bolstered morale and, if they had disrupted business as usual on the streets of Toronto, applied pressure on the employer to settle the dispute on favourable terms.

For those familiar with the record of top officers in CUPE 79 and 416, this failure to prepare for the strike or provide effective direction to win it once it began did not come as a surprise. Both locals have long been led by officers known for their allergy to membership mobilization and clearly left-wing politics.[21] One former member who was fired as a result of his determined union activism once described Local 79 as "very passive and very reluctant to engage in struggle."[22] It is known for "really bureaucratic... management-style unionism," with a leadership that does not foster involvement and is happy "to be able to run the local without the interference of the membership."[23] In 2002, the executive committee's resistance to mobilization and insistence on tightly controlling union affairs led to the resignation of almost the entire strike committee just months before a strike by Locals 79 and 416 that was ended by back-to-work legislation.[24] Although the Local 79 executive board had agreed to the strike committee's report, which proposed an "activist-based strategy" based on beginning mobilization months before a strike, the executive committee of top officers "would not abide by it" (White and Barnett 2002: 27). In 2009, the top officers of the two large Toronto municipal CUPE locals appeared convinced that negotiations would end in a settlement without a strike because they had spent a considerable amount of money and mobilized many volunteers to support the 2003 election and 2006 re-election of David Miller to the mayor's office as well as backing city councillors aligned with Miller.

Enthusiastic support for Miller, an NDP member until 2007 (Byers 2007), was certainly not limited to the leaders of CUPE 79 and 416, but extended across the officers, staff and activists of many unions. A month and a half before the strike began — but when employer demands for a host of concessions from Locals 79 and 416 were on the bargaining table (*CUPE Joint Bargaining News* 2009) — Miller was welcomed at the Stewards' Assembly organized by the Toronto and York Region Labour Council (TYRLC) and attended by some 1600 union activists and officials. The mayor was also featured in TYRLC's glossy brochure commemorating the event (TYRLC 2009b). Those present at the assembly promised to "Work Hard to Renew Solidarity," endorsing a Solidarity Checklist that said, in part, "Just looking after our own members will not be enough to get us through these difficult times. Wage standards, benefits, pensions — when they are taken away from anyone we are all at risk. Helping each other in key struggles will be essential if we want to uphold the quality of life in greater Toronto" (TYRLC 2009b: 7).

The municipal workers' strike was nothing if not a key struggle. Yet most union leaders in Toronto did not treat it as such. There was a "lack of concerted mobilization efforts" (Barnett and Fanelli 2009: 27). TYRLC president John Cartwright's ties with the mayor and his supporters on city council were one reason why the TYRLC leadership did not do everything possible to help win the strike. The suggestion that another activist assembly be convened went unheeded. Desperate for a "friend in city hall," too many in Toronto labour chose to remember only Miller's rhetoric about social justice and not, for example, his 2006 pledge to continue to cut municipal business taxes "every year for the next 15" (Miller 2006). Despite the leading role on Miller's 2003 and 2006 election teams of Conservative organizers including John Laschinger and Liberal insiders such as Peter Donolo (*Globe and Mail* 2005), few in the city's unions recognized him for what he was: a wily politician who welcomed their support but had no intention of taking the side of the working class in Toronto. During the strike, he "attempted to pit City workers against those in the most poverty-stricken and destitute living conditions" (Barnett and Fanelli 2009: 28). As two observers wrote perceptively:

> While dependent upon the local union movement and progressive forces for much of their social base and electoral viability, Miller and the progressive wing of City Council has an alliance with — and even greater fiscal and economic dependence upon — major corporate and financial interests, including many of Canada and North America's most powerful corporations. (Albo and Rosenfeld 2009)

In addition to demonstrating that many in Toronto's unions had worked hard to elect a mayor and councillors who proved willing to provoke a strike to extract concessions from the city's CUPE locals (not one of the labour-backed councillors broke ranks to support the unions), the strike revealed much about the state of the working-class movement. Although the striking unions were not lacking in numbers, money or strike experience — Local 79 had struck in 2000 and both locals had struck at the same time in 2002 — both were notably ineffective.

The top officers and staff of the locals, committed at best to a timid and conventional contract unionism, had not readied members for a fight. Nor had they done much to build unity between members of the two locals and their various bargaining units. Trained in the routines of grievance handling, arbitration, meetings with managers, union administration and campaigning for "friendly" politicians, they proved utterly unable to formulate a strategy for victory, devise creative tactics, motivate members and make a compelling case to other workers about why they should support the strike. Instead, they ran the strike as if the strikers themselves mattered little and the rest of Toronto's working class was irrelevant, squandering the most important potential sources of union power.

For their part, many rank-and-file strikers displayed much endurance and loyalty to the unions despite the poor quality of leadership on offer from top union officers. There were also many indications of how workers were affected by belonging to unions that operate in routinized bureaucratic ways, discourage membership involvement, and do little to educate and mobilize members. Striking workers did not act as an articulate force to try to influence what other people thought about the struggle and the issues at stake. Picket lines were often token, passive and dispirited. At sites where both locals had picket lines, there were sometimes tensions between members of Locals 79 and 416. Aside from a handful of isolated acts of militancy, there were very few independent initiatives by striking workers during the dispute.[25]

The morale of striking municipal workers was no doubt affected by their isolation from most of the rest of the working class in Toronto. The strike revealed just how many workers, feeling acutely insecure about their own jobs and fearful of how the economic crisis would affect them and their families, were quick to respond with hostility to public sector workers defending past gains. As Walkom put it, "Hard times breed class resentment. Unfortunately, the wrong class usually gets targeted." Rather than directing anger at employers and at governments that cater to capitalists' demands for higher profits, "we have found a more convenient group of people upon whom we can vent our fear and frustration. They're closer. They're easier to beat up" (Walkom 2009).

This kind of response is not natural or automatic. It stems from the reality that wage-earners are set against each other in competition in labour markets in capitalist societies. The attitudes that led so many Torontonians to blame the city's workforce for the strike have also been actively cultivated by the dominant ways of understanding society during the neoliberal era. For years, most politicians, journalists, academics and other "experts" whose opinions are carried through the corporate news and entertainment media have repeated time and again that workers must give up past gains. The onset of a global economic crisis in 2008 only made such calls more emphatic, even though workers' wages and benefits did not cause the crisis. People have been constantly encouraged to think of themselves as taxpayers. This identity conceals both divisions between classes and the fact that most "taxpayers" are members of the working class who share common interests. But years of increased insecurity in people's lives and saturation in neoliberal ideology — with little resistance from most unions or other social movements or political forces — have had a real impact on the working class. Basic social solidarity has been corroded. Many people react with anger at those who seek to defend rights, benefits or wages that are better than what they themselves enjoy, rather than wishing them well. Although the strike was not without support in the region, it was the hostile response that was strongest in Toronto during the summer of 2009.

It was not only CUPE 79 and 416 that did little to challenge people to respond in a different way. As mentioned, the leadership of the TYRLC, the umbrella organization of the city's unions, did not act and speak as if the strike was a key struggle, although they did help to ensure that a range of unions brought some of their members to CUPE picket lines.[26] In general, the efforts to organize solidarity did not convey a sense of how important this strike was: a high-profile, large-scale test of the ability of public sector unions to resist the stepping-up of the employers' offensive that followed the beginning of the recession and had fallen hardest on private sector unions.

Strikes can be "schools of struggle" — important experiences that change those involved. When people stop work and can see the impact of doing so, they get a taste of working-class power. Strikes can demonstrate that a collective rather than individual response to problems is not only possible, but more effective for working people. Because strikes make the class antagonism between workers and employers so clear, they often create possibilities for workers to bridge divisions among themselves, such as those between people with different ethno-racial identities or whose jobs require different levels of formal education. By taking a stand and organizing strike activities, strikers can develop self-confidence, overcoming fears and old beliefs about what ordinary people are unable to do. Illusions about benevolent employers and governments and about the state as a neutral force can be dispelled.

However, this strike did not teach such lessons. It could only be demoralizing to spend weeks picketing with almost no information about what was happening in bargaining or on other picket lines, with no inkling of a strategy to try to bring the strike to a successful end, and without ideas and inspiration to challenge hostile claims and encourage perseverance. Deprived of any opportunity to democratically shape how the strike would be run, Toronto municipal workers were given no reason to think of their unions as *their* organizations. Nor did the strike bring municipal workers and other sections of the working class in the city closer together — far from it. "The strike was a political failure when it came to mobilizing sustained action and education, garnering public support as well as linking the defense of unionized jobs with fighting for workers in non-unionized jobs, the underemployed and the unemployed" (Barnett and Fanelli 2009: 28–29). This made it easier for right-wing populist candidate Rob Ford to channel "concerns about particular public services against city workers, and the idea of the public sector as a whole" (Saberi and Kipfer 2010) as part of his successful run to become the mayor of Toronto in 2010. It is possible in some circumstances for a strike that ends in defeat to nevertheless lead to a stronger union. For this to happen, enough members must gain hard-won insights and emerge with new resolve to become actively involved so the defeat will not be repeated. A strike that ends in defeat can also produce stronger class solidarity if it has a lasting impact on people who identified with and supported the struggle. This was not such a strike. It did not generate a new commitment among strikers to union involvement. Nor did it build unity and solidarity in the working class in Canada's largest city. But it does tell us a great deal about the challenges facing the workers' movement.

Notes

1. Much of my understanding of the working-class movement has been shaped by personal observation, participation and discussion with labour activists (to whom I owe an enormous debt, far more than is reflected in this book's references) over two decades, for which it is impossible to provide references.
2. E-mail from Will Offley to author, May 16, 2008. Offley is a veteran labour activist, most recently in the BCNU.
3. Interview with Shellie Bird, May 31, 2009. Bird is a CUPE activist who at the time of the interview was a member of the executive board of CUPE Ontario.
4. Nova Scotia union officer, personal communication, July 28, 2009.
5. Interview with Will Offley, February 14, 2009.
6. Interview with Karen Naylor, January 9, 2009. Naylor was for many years a local officer and then a staff representative in the Canadian Brotherhood of Railway, Transport and General Workers, which merged with the CAW in 1995.
7. Interview with John Friesen, November 19, 2008.
8. Interview with Russ St. Eloi, February 18, 2009. St. Eloi is a long-time elected official in the Plumbers and Pipefitters union.
9. Unpublished data provided by the Strategic Policy, Analysis and Workplace Information Directorate of Human Resources and Skills Development Canada.
10. The inclusion of agricultural wage-labourers, who are currently still barred from unionizing in Ontario and Alberta, would lower this percentage slightly. On the other hand, the non-agricultural paid workforce measured by Statistics Canada includes people who are not part of the working class even in the broad definition used in this book, such as high-ranking managerial personnel. Another technical issue is that there are people who are covered by union contracts but are not union members. This includes workers in unionized workplaces who exercise their right not to join the union, some probationary employees and some supervisors. In 1999, they accounted for 7.4 percent of those covered by collective agreements (Akyeampong 2000). In 2009, adding such persons yielded a total of 31.6 percent of non-agricultural employees covered by a collective agreement (Statistics Canada 2009), about 2 percent higher than the figure for union membership.
11. In 2001, union density for workers of colour was 21.3 percent. The number of workers who identified themselves as members of a "visible minority" was 9.3 percent, but only 6.9 percent of unionized workers identified themselves as such. Aboriginal workers were counted as 2.7 percent of both all wage-earners and all unionized workers, with a density rate of 30.4 percent, but this measures only indigenous people living off-reserve and probably undercounts urban indigenous workers (Jackson and Schetagne 2004: 81). Cheung (2006: 30) reports a union density rate for workers of colour in 2003 of roughly 21 percent. More recent data is not available.
12. Unpublished data provided by the Strategic Policy, Analysis and Workplace Information Directorate of Human Resources and Skills Development Canada, 2009.

13. The website www.uncharted.ca created by dissident UFCW members contains material on the UFCW from a critical point of view.
14. The agreement was ratified by two-thirds of the CUPW membership, but opposed by most of the union's activists, which at the next CUPW convention led to the defeat of the incumbent National President, Deborah Bourque, who had recommended the deal, by Denis Lemelin, an NEB opponent of the contract.
15. Interview with Karen Naylor, January 9, 2009.
16. Author's calculation, from data in Statistics Canada 2009.
17. Data from the website of the Labour Program of Human Resources and Skills Development Canada <hrsdc.gc.ca/eng/labour/labour_relations/info_analysis/work_stoppages/index.shtml>.
18. E-mail from Julia Barnett to author, June 28, 2009. Barnett is a shop steward and long-time activist in Toronto CUPE municipal public sector union locals.
19. Julia Barnett to author, telephone communication, August 23, 2009.
20. Zerbisias 2009 was an exception.
21. CUPE 79 disaffiliated from CUPE's Ontario Division in 2008. This move was the culmination of longstanding tensions between top officers of Local 79 and the more left-wing top officers of the Division.
22. Interview with Stan Dalton, 2003. Dalton was an active shop steward in CUPE 79.
23. Interview with CUPE 79 activists A2 and A3, May 2004.
24. Interview with CUPE 79 activist A4, May 17, 2004.
25. These observations are informed by conversations during the strike with CUPE 79 activist Claudia White, a member of CUPE 79 who prefers anonymity and CUPE 1281 member Sheila Wilmot.
26. For example, the TYRLC statement "Message to City Hall — Only a Fair Contract Will Settle the Strike" (TYRLC 2009a) noted that "there is a real danger of a backlash being exploited by the right-wing and corporate interests in this city" and warned that "Mayor Miller and the progressive Councillors who enjoyed labour's support would do well to understand the political minefield that is being sown every day that the strike continues." But it was silent about the significance of the strike *for workers* in the city and across Canada and Quebec, especially public sector workers. The statement gives the impression that the TYRLC leadership was more concerned about how the strike would affect its "friends" in City Hall — politicians who were actively or passively backing an attack on two TYRLC affiliates! — than anything else.

2. Union Activity Beyond the Contract

The activities examined in the last chapter — enforcing, administering, bargaining and defending collective agreements — occupy most of the energies of unions today. All legal strikes are connected to the defence or improvement of contracts. But union activities today also include organizing non-unionized workers into unions, labour-community campaigns, international solidarity and political action, education and equality-promoting work. These are the focus of this chapter.

Organizing

"Organize the unorganized!" is an old union slogan. Yet, rhetoric aside, reaching out to organize non-union workers is a high priority for few unions in Canada. In most cases, this kind of activity involves union organizing staff working with pro-union workers. At times, unionized worker volunteers from other workplaces are brought in to help with union drives. Active campaigns to assist workers to organize into unions do continue to happen. However, the scale of organizing has been falling since the mid-1980s (Jackson 2006: 66). The organizing that is taking place is "not enough to counter the ongoing loss of union jobs from economic restructuring and the fact that job growth in the private sector is concentrated in mainly non-union sectors and occupations" (61), both of which are nibbling away at union density. The problem is not just one of scale, but also of how unions approach organizing the unorganized. While there are examples of organizing efforts that seriously take into account how sexism and racism affect workers' lives inside and outside the workplace and patiently aim to foster democratic collective organization among workers from the beginning (for example, the United Steel Workers' [USW] success at the Omega Direct call centre in Sudbury [Guard, Steedman and Garcia-Orgales 2007]), most union drives do not (Wilmot 2008a).

An extreme case of a bid for more members regardless of the kind of union this builds is the CAW-Magna deal. In 2007, CAW leaders signed the Framework of Fairness Agreement (FFA) with the Canadian-based multinational auto parts firm Magna International, a notoriously anti-union employer. The FFA commits Magna to allow workers to vote on joining the CAW under a collective agreement drawn up without workers' input. The contract denies Magna workers the right to strike when it expires and a standard grievance procedure. The FFA commits the CAW to collaborate with the employer's agenda of productivity and profitability. In addition, workers organized into the CAW under the FFA do not elect shop stewards and local union officers (Gindin 2007; Rosenfeld 2007; Bickerton 2007). The FFA drew widespread criticism from both local activists and top officers (Fraser et al. 2007) of other unions as well as from some CAW activists, but has attracted few Magna workers to unionization (Rosenfeld 2008a). Rather than being the first move in a different direction, the FFA has flopped even on its own terms. Another attempt to find a short cut around grassroots worker organizing and employer opposition to unions, the USW's 2008 move to organize long-time non-union Hamilton steel firm Dofasco, went down in flames. USW officials relied on a neutrality deal — which commits the employer to not oppose a union drive — and failed to consider how workers would respond to what seemed "a done deal arranged over their heads" (Humphrey 2008).

Labour and "the Community"

Organizing workers without union representation is obviously connected directly to unions' central focus on contracts. This is not the case with union involvement in what is usually called "the community:" charities, non-profit organizations, activist groups and the like. Many union locals take part in United Way campaigns and other charitable fund-raising efforts. Higher-level union structures, whose officers have access to greater financial resources than local officers, make donations to many groups and causes. Unions provide financial and volunteer support for federal, provincial and local groups that educate and lobby for public health care, against privatization and around poverty, human rights and other issues. Less often, some unions attempt to mobilize members to participate in demonstrations and other actions against social injustice. Union support of any kind for activist groups that use militant tactics, such as the Ontario Coalition Against Poverty (OCAP), was always small-scale and has fallen significantly since the right-ward shift in the political climate following the terrorist attacks of September 11, 2001.[1] Labour-community cooperation is often fraught with tensions stemming from the different ways of operating, political outlooks and experiences of union and community activists. Another point of contention is unions' greater financial resources. In the words of one movement activist, unions often "implicitly say: 'We have the resources, and you must respect our needs and priorities if you want to access them'" (Rosenfeld 2008b: 37). Overall, the level of activity by unions with community groups that goes beyond making donations and encouraging charitable giving is minimal.

One high-profile exception is Toronto's labour council. Labour councils are made up of delegates from locals affiliated to the Canadian Labour

Congress (CLC) in a given city or region. While some labour councils barely function or have folded in recent years,[2] the TYRLC leadership has sought to revitalize the organization, drawing on the experiences of labour councils in a few major U.S. cities (TYRLC n.d.). Activities organized in conjunction with social service agencies and organizations with real roots in communities of colour have been central to its efforts. The TYRLC's 2007 campaign to raise Ontario's minimum wage involved print and online petitions and public meetings in multiracial lower-income neighbourhoods (Wilmot 2008b).

Even in such cases, it is rare for union activists who do "labour-community" work to consciously understand that most of the people lumped together as "the community" are part of the working class, including non-unionized wage earners, the unwaged and union members active in neighbourhood, religious, ethno-cultural and other groups. Middle-class elements like small business owners, lawyers, doctors and managers make up only a small proportion of "the community." It is also uncommon for unions whose members provide services that directly affect many people — for example, in public transit, teaching and health care — to approach collective bargaining with a strategy for building the active support of service users. This could involve raising demands for better services and building an alliance with people outside the union who support these demands, using tactics like transit workers refusing to collect fares from passengers. Toronto's 2009 municipal strike was a prime example of unions not doing this. Similarly, unions almost never approach joint work with organizations based outside the workplace from a perspective of building the unity and power of the working class across the division between unionized and non-unionized workers and across the different spheres in which workers live their lives: paid workplaces, households and communities.

International Work

Related to union activity with "the community" is union international work. The national offices of most major unions in Canada and Quebec include departments whose staff are responsible for international affairs. Most major unions also maintain a fund used to support international projects. Some unions have committees that involve officers and other active members in international work. Today, most unions' policies on global affairs are moderately progressive in their formal opposition to neoliberal policies, war and the domination of the Global South, including Canada's role in the occupation of Afghanistan (Bickerton 2006; Weisleder 2005). Unfortunate exceptions include the support by the top leaders of some Quebec unions for the 2004 coup in Haiti engineered by the governments of the U.S., Canada and France and the regime installed by the coup (Engler 2008; Engler and Fenton 2005). The most common pattern is for unions to adopt mildly left-wing policies on international issues that — like so many union policy statements — then remain dead letters. Union financial donations most often go to emergency relief for people in countries of the South, to development projects or to sustain Non-Governmental Organizations (NGOs). Like most union "community" efforts within Canada and Quebec, this can be characterized as charity — giving aid to the needy, rather than supporting the efforts of people to organize themselves to struggle for change — even when it is talked about in the language of solidarity.

But some union work is genuinely international working-class solidarity that supports movements fighting for change. Notable here is assistance to campaigns against privatization and in support of unionists in Colombia who are targeted by that country's repressive government and the death squads linked to it. Most of this work directly touches few union members in Canada and Quebec. An exception to this has been the extensive work by CUPE-Ontario International Solidarity Committee activists to educate people about the politics and history of Israel and Palestine as part of CUPE-Ontario's support for the campaign for Boycott, Divestment and Sanctions against Israel in solidarity with the Palestinian freedom struggle. This educational effort, which has trained rank-and-file members as educators, conducted dozens of presentations in cities and towns across the province, distributed thousands of booklets and built links between unionists and community-based Palestine solidarity activists, has reached thousands of CUPE members — more than in any previous CUPE-Ontario campaign.[3]

When it comes to actually crossing borders, most unions send a handful of loyal officers or staff to international conferences. A few do more, such as organizing solidarity visits and speakers' tours (for some examples, see Bocking 2007 and Schwartz 2009b).

Political Action[4]

Another kind of union activity beyond contract bargaining and enforcement is "political action." This is generally understood to mean parliamentary politics: efforts to elect candidates to federal, provincial or municipal office and to influence politicians. Outside of election campaigns, the CLC, its provincial and local bodies, other labour centrals, and many unions use the conventional channels for attempting to influence governments, including lobbying, presenting briefs to committees, postcard campaigns and the like. Unions sometimes mount court challenges to pieces of legislation they oppose. They also provide crucial funding for the Canadian Centre for Policy Alternatives, a think tank critical of neoliberal policies.

The greatest effort goes into supporting a political party at election time. Outside Quebec, this is usually the New Democratic Party (NDP). At its foundation in 1961, the NDP was a social democratic party independent of corporations and closely aligned with unions, so much so that it can be seen as a component of the working-class movement in Canada at the time (the NDP never managed to develop significant support in Quebec). Unions based in manufacturing industries were the strongest NDP supporters, "whereas construction and public sector unions were more ambivalent in their political alliances" (Yates 2008: 90). Over the last decade of the twentieth century and into the twenty-first, the NDP — like social democratic parties in other advanced capitalist countries — has changed considerably. In a process that has unfolded unevenly across the provinces and at the level of the federal party, the NDP has abandoned traditional social democratic policies of social reform within capitalism and accommodated or even embraced neoliberalism. Over the same period, the NDP's roots in unions and the working class more broadly have grown weaker (Cooke 2007; Savage 2010). The NDP still draws much support from unionists, but it is questionable whether the party still represents any form of working-class politics independent of corporate power.

Some unions never supported the NDP. In Canada, some craft unions and nurses' and teachers' unions have long backed federal and provincial Liberals. In Quebec, most of the labour officialdom believes its close ties with the leaders of the Parti Québécois (PQ) and Bloc Québécois (BQ) — nationalist parties that have cultivated both union and corporate support, not parties linked with unions as the NDP was in its early years — allows labour to advance its interests. Union officers lead Syndicalistes et Progressistes pour un Québec Libre (SPQ Libre), a club that promoted social democratic politics within the now-neoliberal PQ until it was expelled by the PQ leadership in 2010 (Radio-Canada 2010). A small number of union officers and rank-and-file activists have swung behind the small left-wing pro-independence party Québéc Solidaire (QS).

Outside Quebec, as the NDP has moved rightward and its leaders put more distance between themselves and unions, the ties between some of the unions aligned with the NDP and the party have loosened. With political horizons lowered and no left-wing political alternative to the NDP on offer, some unions have drawn closer to the Liberals. This is evidence of "a union movement in retreat, desperate to hold on to its post-war gains, in the face of a neoliberal assault on labour" (Savage 2010: 23). The CAW is the starkest example. The CAW has shifted away from its traditional "unwavering support" (Allen 2006: 18) for the NDP to a policy, when faced with Conservative governments, of backing "winnable" NDP candidates, Liberal candidates in other ridings in Canada and BQ candidates in Quebec. "The spectacle in December 2005 of CAW National President Buzz Hargrove gleefully giving then Prime Minister Paul Martin a CAW jacket to wear while Martin was campaigning for re-election" (18) was only a high-profile moment in the CAW's drawing closer to the federal and Ontario provincial Liberals (Hargrove was expelled from the NDP for his stance).

Changes to federal party finance legislation that took effect in 2004 have altered how unions support parties, above all the NDP, which no longer accepts donations by unions to its candidates, campaigns or riding associations. What has not changed is that most unions rely on parliamentary politics as the main way to influence government. Union staff can take unpaid leave to work on an election campaign and union members can volunteer; many unions encourage their members and staff to devote time to the party supported by the union. Unions produce flyers, advertisements, websites and other material designed to persuade unionists and members of their families to vote for a particular party, although the party may not be named explicitly. For example, in the 2006 federal election, the CLC ran a campaign under the slogan "Better Choices." Its brochure did not explicitly name any party, while CUPE's 2006 "Vote Positive, Vote Public" brochure criticized the Liberals and Conservatives and praised the NDP. In the end, efforts to encourage union members to vote for the NDP have never had a major impact: "Electoral studies have repeatedly shown that union members, while more likely to vote NDP than non-union workers, are most likely to vote Liberal in federal elections" (Yates 2008: 90).

In municipal elections, where candidates usually do not run as members of a political party, unions typically back candidates perceived as less hostile to unions, regardless of whether they also have corporate backers — as in the cases of Toronto's David Miller and the municipal Vision Vancouver party — or have no corporate ties. This approach reveals most clearly the way so many union officers, staff and activists now relate to politics in general, not just municipal elections. Political action has become, as Stephanie Ross has aptly described it, a matter of "choosing the least bad of the present political options" rather than "trying to construct a real workers' alternative" (Ross 2009). Basic principles like workers' need for politics independent of capitalists in order to defend and advance their interests — a hallmark of much union political activism in the twentieth century, whether in support of social democracy or a radical left-wing perspective — have often been jettisoned. The result is often an unprincipled "politics of pragmatism" that "can lead unions to some perverse, often conservative, political positions that erode their long-term viability" (Yates 2008: 103). Examples of such positions include union support for municipal politicians like Miller and those of Vision Vancouver, federal and provincial Liberals and the NDP, where it is no longer independent of major corporations. Uncritical union support for the bid late in 2008 to form a federal coalition government — in reality, a Liberal government in which the NDP would have played a subordinate role — also demonstrated a desperate grasping for what was perceived as "the least bad" option. The logical conclusion of support for such a government would be the liquidation of the NDP into the Liberals and the abandonment of any pretense of union political action independent of the two traditional parties of the Canadian ruling class, the Liberals and Conservatives.

Since the mid-1970s, the capitalist assault on workers and unions and the inability of the established methods of parliamentary political action to stop it have pushed unions to sporadically use extra-parliamentary methods of political action that had almost disappeared from the movement after the late 1940s, except in Quebec. The most common tactic is public protest in the streets: demonstrations, rallies and marches. Often, these are one-time-only affairs rather than part of escalating campaigns of action. As such, they represent a kind of highly visible mass lobbying of government. Protests of this type can also be a way for union officials to signal to their members that they are taking an issue seriously, thereby avoiding the charge that they are doing nothing. Less often, such actions have been undertaken as part of a sustained mobilization, as in the case of the mass demonstrations that were part of the Days of Action held in different Ontario cities against the province's Conservative government between 1995 and 1999 (Camfield 2000). Public union protest is sometimes organized in support of an ongoing strike to express solidarity with the strikers and pressure a government or private employer to meet the strike's demands. For example, actions of this kind took place in support of the teachers' strike in B.C. in October 2005, a widely-backed strike that also saw other public sector workers defy the law to strike in support of the teachers (Camfield 2009a). Unions have also mobilized members for demonstrations that they have endorsed or organized in conjunction with other groups, including protests against global injustice and war, student rallies against tuition increases and anti-poverty actions. However, this kind of mobilization has become less frequent in recent years. When unions do organize public protests, symbolic actions (such as rallies or tightly regulated marches) are much more common than militant mass direct action (such as taking to the streets without a permit or occupying a building). Unions may also go on strike outside of collective bargaining to protest government actions. Ontario teachers walked off the job for two weeks in 1997 in opposition to provincial legislation. Many of the Days of Action in Ontario involved work stoppages and protests on a Friday followed by large marches and rallies the following day. Political strikes also took place as part of the anti-government Days of Defiance organized in Duncan and Victoria, B.C., in 2002. Quebec unions held a Day of Disruption in December 2003 that saw many workers strike.

In general, though, extra-parliamentary action by unions and its influence on political discussions among union activists peaked between 1995 and 2001 and has since waned. For example, as a now-retired long-time paperworker union activist observed, neither "the movement's formal leadership" nor "any visible sector" of members was present alongside anti-poverty and indigenous rights activists in protests against the 2010 Olympics on the streets of Vancouver (McGuckin 2010).[5] This decline has had a noticeable effect on unions. When extra-parliamentary politics brings people together in collective action on a large scale, it can give workers a sense of their power that can be exhilarating, much like an effective strike against an employer. When this happens, people begin to change how they think about themselves, their organizations and the possibility of changing society. This was dramatically evident among union members who were involved in the large militant global justice protests that took place around the summit held to negotiate a Free Trade Area of the Americas in Quebec City in 2001. This was one of the experiences that was beginning, in some regions, to foster the formation of small flying squads and other networks of union activists attracted to solidarity with other struggles and to more militant action (Kuhling and Levant 2006; Sears 2001). The decline of extra-parliamentary politics led to the dissipation of these emerging activist networks. It has also made electoral politics seem like the only option for unions. Working on election campaigns may encourage unionized workers to think about issues beyond their own immediate workplaces, but voting in elections does nothing to build workers' collective power. Electoral support for the "least bad" does not foster even the limited kind of "us vs. them" working-class consciousness that support for the union-linked social democratic NDP against the Bay Street-backed Liberals and Tories used to do. In fact, it does the opposite. Encouraging unionized workers to vote for parties or candidates backed by parts of the employing class erodes the foundation of unionism: the recognition that the interests of workers and employers are fundamentally different.

Education

Educational courses and workshops are another aspect of what unions do. Involving perhaps as many as 120,000 members annually, the education offered by unions, the CLC, provincial federations of labour and some labour councils aims to teach members how to be active in the sometimes-complex world of union organization, familiarize them with the legal, policy and other dimensions of the environment in which unions operate and foster union consciousness. Most union education is focused on "tools" related to workplace rights (such as how to be a shop steward or a member of a bargaining team or health and safety committee). Some deals with "issues" (for example, racism). A smaller number of courses look at broader economic and political questions. Union education is now often influenced, to some extent, by popular education methods that stress the importance of workers' experiences and knowledge rather than the techniques of traditional classroom schooling

(Taylor 2001; Wilmot 2009: 46–52). The ideology of the officialdom of the organization offering the education is generally reflected in the content of courses. For example, CUPW education is distinctly more left-wing and critical of employers and capitalism than that offered to UFCW members, while the TYRLC's Labour Education Centre uses an anti-oppression perspective that looks at class, race and gender. For a minority of people exposed to it, union education provides an introduction to critical ways of understanding society that are almost never on offer in other forms of adult education or in the corporate media. Yet even union education that promotes a critical perspective on society, encourages members to work for social change and advocates equality for people who experience oppression rarely raises questions about how unions themselves function today (Wilmot 2009: 52), such as how the law forces unionized workers to rely on the grievance and arbitration system to deal with workplace problems.

Working for Equality

A final area of union activity, apart from the tasks related to directly negotiating and enforcing collective agreements, is equity work. This term covers activities that aim to tackle forms of oppression (systemic discrimination) that exist in society and therefore among workers and within unions: the sexism experienced by women, racism against people of colour and indigenous people, heterosexism targeting lesbian, gay, bisexual and transgender (LGBT) people and the systemic discrimination encountered by people with disabilities. As a result of the hard work of activists, many unions have internal structures for one form or another of equity work. Many national unions have a handful of staffers assigned to work against one or more of these forms of oppression, as do the major union centrals. Some locals and other union bodies have women's committees or caucuses (caucuses are solely open to members of an oppressed group). Less often, and under various names, there are committees or caucuses for other groups of people who experience specific forms of oppression. When such structures exist, what they do varies widely. Activities include educating union members and staff about oppression, advocating for equity proposals to take to the bargaining table and pushing for changes aimed at reducing the dominance of able-bodied straight white men in elected and appointed positions within unions (such as courses in union education programs and designated seats on executive boards for members of equity-seeking groups). Some union equity-type committees work with activist groups outside unions (Foley and Baker 2009; Hunt and Rayside 2007; Wilmot 2005: 117–22).

However, despite "policies designed to remove discrimination and bias... good intentions have not necessarily been diffused to the local level" (Hunt and Haiven 2006: 678). The problem is not just at the level of union locals, either. It is also clear that good intentions — which are not enough to make action against oppression effective — have not permeated the union officialdom above the local level. Where good policies exist, they are often not implemented.[6] CUPW staff person Marion Pollack worries that "acknowledging the issues facing women, lesbian, gay, and trans people, workers of colour, differently abled workers, and Indigenous workers is increasingly becoming lip service" (Pollack 2010: 26). What Sheila Wilmot writes about official policies for anti-racist work in CUPE can be said more generally about equity policies and structures in unions today: "It is not clear... with what longevity and how consistently this translates into action and supports rank-and-file organizing at the local level" (Wilmot 2005: 119). This raises the issue of what goes on inside unions, an important question taken up in the next chapter.

Notes

1. Interview with John Clarke, June 10, 2009. Clarke was a founder of OCAP and since its inception has been one of its central organizers. Prior to that, he was a union activist in Britain and then in Canada.
2. Interview with Atlantic labour staffer, July 10, 2009.
3. Information drawn from an untitled 2008 document by Katherine Nastovski (copy in author's possession).
4. This section draws on Camfield 2008.
5. See Nelson 2010 for discussion of union support for the Vancouver Olympics.
6. Interview with Carol Wall, June 12, 2009. Wall was a CEP activist who became a CEP staff representative and then the CEP's first Human Rights director. She was elected as a CLC Vice-President representing workers of colour in 2002 and ran a dissident campaign for the presidency of the CLC in 2005. She later worked for the PSAC.

3. Inside the Unions: Organizational Life

The first two chapters of this book have looked at different activities under-taken in unions today. It is also important to specifically examine how unions operate and what they are like as organizations. Although we often say that unions, like other organizations, do things, this is misleading. "What does it mean to say that 'the union' adopts a particular policy or carries out a certain action? This is a clear instance of... reification: treating an impersonal abstraction as a social agent, when it is really only people who act" (Hyman 1975: 16). Unions do not act. Unions are organizations through which people act in a range of ways. To understand how this happens in Canada and Quebec today, we need to look at several questions: Who carries out union activities? How are decisions made, and by whom? How do the realities of privilege and oppression in society shape unions? How do we make sense of the different approaches that union members and staff take towards what unions should do and what unionism means?

Members, Officers and Staff

Millions of wage earners in Canada and Quebec are represented by unions. But most union members are not active in their unions most of the time. The level of membership activism varies widely across unions and within locals of the same union. In general, though, many activists report that the level of membership involvement has fallen in recent years. When "there's not stuff happening either in the streets or in their workplaces in terms of workplace action" and a "lower level of overall militancy... there is not a lot to drive folks out into meetings."[1]

The approach taken by a union's staff, officers (members who have been elected or appointed to executive boards and other bodies) and active rank-and-filers (members who do not hold any union position) can certainly influence the level of membership activity. There are different attitudes across unions to key questions such as: should activism be encouraged? If so, how? What should it look like? But when not much is going on, participation will be low and few people will be motivated to become union activists. Most unionized workers will only become personally involved when union activity affects them very directly, such as when a tentative agreement has been negotiated and workers have their chance to vote to ratify or reject it, or when a strike or lock-out seems likely. At other times, union activity is carried out by union staff, officers and other volunteer members of the rank-and-file.

Most unions hire their staff, often from their own memberships, but also from the outside. A partial exception to this is CUPW: some staff positions in this union are filled by electing members for a fixed term of office rather than through a hiring procedure. In most unions, the majority of stewards and local executive board members receive no money for their service. But many contracts allow stewards and certain officers some paid time off work to carry out union business. A minority of officers are full-timers; that is, they perform union work on a full-time basis. Although top full-time officers and staff generally act as key leaders in unions, many thousands of members regularly carry out union activity in the workplace or serve on committees. All these volunteers usually go unnoticed by outside observers, but are absolutely vital for unions. They are also a much larger group than the activist base of any other social movement.[2]

The fact that some of these active members get some paid time off work and some officers serve as full-timers makes it considerably easier for union activity to get done, since most wage-earners live busy lives. At the same time, these arrangements also create complications. As a retired CAW staffer argues:

> There's a hierarchy in the unions of people who have sort of privileges: they get to take time off work, they get paid for lots of stuff.... I find that model takes away from the membership actually being active. You have an active local leadership, but it can... be a bit self-serving.... The people in the local leadership don't want to go back on the floor.[3]

It is not always the case that activists use union work as a way to escape their workplaces. Many stewards and local officers are self-sacrificing volunteers. Nevertheless, even principled activists who devote countless hours of their time to fighting for their fellow workers can get used to being able to leave the workplace to perform union tasks or attend conferences — activities they may find more meaningful than their regular jobs. As a result, they can become attached to their union positions for self-interested reasons. If this is true of selfless activists, it is even more true for union members with less commitment to principles. Careerists can and do use paid union service as a means of personal advancement, with the goal of getting a full-time union position or even crossing over to a job in the employer's human resources department. This problem is most common in unions in which prospective leaders are rarely tested in democratic organizing and debate.[4]

The role of staff is another source of problems. In many unions, staff wield enormous influence. This comes at the expense of the democratic control of unions by their members. That said, staff domination usually has its limits. For example, "typically Steelworker staff controlled the union, [and] still do to a major extent." Yet the amalgamation of many small USW locals into larger locals as a "cost-saving measure" has ended up weakening "the old levers of control" used by staff representatives; as local officers are forced to take on more responsibilities, they demand more say.[5] In CUPE, the situation is "very diverse." According to a critical-minded CUPE staffer, some "staff reps… take over too many authorities and roles from what I think are the rightful roles of local elected people." Such staff have a "not very democratic orientation," but there is also a "structural problem": many staff representatives carry enormous workloads. This creates "an inclination to reach, find and then ratify an easy [bargaining] settlement that may not be very good, as opposed to strategizing around a more effective or stronger or more militant fight that would produce a better settlement." In CUPE — as in other unions — the problem is generally more complex than staff simply usurping control from members. Members have often become so accustomed to staffers doing the bulk of union work that they expect staff to do this — after all, some members say, "that is why they are paid so much money."[6] The result in many unions is "a huge dependence on staff."[7] At least CUPE's policy that staff are employees of the union, and not also CUPE members, avoids the problem found in some other unions of staff holding memberships in the union they are supposed to serve. When staff are members of the same union they work for, they gain even more influence within it; rank-and-file members' control over their union usually suffers. This can be seen in unions that allow staff to simultaneously hold elected union office, such as the Service Employees International Union (SEIU), or in which staff can move into elected positions, as in the Communications, Energy and Paperworkers (CEP) in which most elected top officers are former staffers.[8]

Another factor that influences who carries out union activity is how active members and staff relate to other members. Do they try to encourage more people to become involved? If they do, does the way they go about union work actually motivate involvement? What are members encouraged to do in the union? A hard-working local president may sincerely repeat that he wants more members to become active in the local, but then not let others take on more responsibility for fear they will "get it wrong." There may be few opportunities for members who are not stewards or on the executive to get involved in a local, or there may be committees or other structures that make it easy to do so.

In fact, in many unions today, officials still have a "leave it to us" attitude. From this perspective, members should allow officials to take care of union business and act only when officials call on them to do so, such as when a vote to authorize a strike is needed to back up the bargaining team at the negotiating table. This attitude is part of the common pattern of unions operating as institutions that provide services to passive members rather than as active workers' organizations. In what is often called the servicing model, "members don't have the opportunity to learn about winning grievances, bargaining or figuring out strategy, and the idea that they need servicing becomes self-fulfilling. As contracts become more and more complicated, the existence of experts is justified" (Parker and Gruelle 1999: 24). Members who are treated as customers by union officials "can easily get stuck between a rational desire to be 'serviced' and the frustration that comes when their hired leaders don't deliver, as happens more and more often" (25). The bottom line, as dissident CAW activist Cathy Austin puts it, is that "not building power with workers, 'taking care' of them instead of helping them to realize their own power, can be a barrier to both organizing and building a strong union" (Austin, Descary and Nastovski 2007: 14).

There are also situations in which militant activists who reject the servicing model fight vigorously on behalf of members, without really changing members' relationship to the union. Both the servicing approach and this kind of fighting *for* members (rather than helping members to act for themselves) are examples of *substitutionism*: a person or group of people acting in ways that do not assist others to act for themselves (in other words, that do not foster their self-activity). Substitutionism is pervasive in unions today. An unusually critical union convention document describes what happens as a result: "The debates and decision-making mechanisms are centralized at the top of the union hierarchy. Consequently, the resulting actions most often circulate top-down and very rarely bottom-up." This "accentuates the feeling of distance between the grassroots and the top" (FIQ 2008: 23).

In unions whose leaders have attempted to move from the servicing model to what is often called the organizing model emphasis is placed on members themselves doing more instead of relying on staff (this may be motivated by a desire to cut back on the number of staff assigned to locals as servicing representatives, by the belief that a more active membership is inherently good because it builds a stronger union or a mixture of both). This kind of shift is not easy. Members may not want to take on more responsibilities, and staff may not want to give them up — for example, one CUPE provincial executive board member notes that in CUPE "there is resistance on the staff around empowering members."[9] In addition, member involvement does not necessarily go along with control. A union in which members become more active but do not have democratic control over their union is one in which substitutionism still exists, even if to a lesser degree.

Union Democracy

Raising the issue of membership control brings us directly to union democracy, how decisions are made and who makes them. Here I use democracy to refer to more than a system in which people vote from time to time to select who will make decisions in their name. By contrast, democracy in its original Greek sense means rule by the poor or by the people including the poor (Wood 1995: 220–23). If we understand democracy in this much more substantial way, in terms of popular power, then union democracy means more than free and fair elections for union offices. It means control by workers over their union organizations.

How democratic, then, are contemporary unions? Union locals are generally rather more democratic than governments; in most unions, elections for local executive boards and other offices are held every year or two and local by-laws often contain provisions that allow members to remove elected officers if the need arises. Elections are usually free and fair, although there are exceptions.[10] By comparison with today's parliamentary system, unions are quite democratic. But this is a low bar. Moreover, frequent elections are no guarantee that workers really will control their unions, although elections are a necessity for democratic unionism. For a union to be highly democratic, members must be able to control union affairs. Union locals that hold frequent meetings open to all members and in which members are able to use these meetings to make important decisions are potentially highly democratic organizations.

The structure of the local can be decisive here. There is currently a trend in some unions, especially some headquartered in the U.S. like the SEIU, UNITE HERE and UFCW, towards creating fewer, larger locals. The starkest example of this is UFCW 175-633 (an unusual joint local, and the largest union local in the country). This local claims a membership of some 50,000 people under nearly 400 collective agreements in about 900 workplaces across Ontario. Larger than some national unions and structured without concern for democracy, its members are, for all intents and purposes, unable to influence the organization beyond each of the nearly sixty areas into which they are divided (each area holds a quarterly membership meeting).[11] Such mega-locals "cannot possibly be democratic in any way," argues Kim Moody in his excellent analysis of U.S. unions in the early twenty-first century. "Whatever formal structures they have, membership control of the central leaders, staff, and resources is impossible in the vast geographic areas they cover." Even if regional membership meetings exist, such regional structures have "little ability to communicate *horizontally* with one another, and no real power over the new administrative centers" (Moody 2007: 194). UFCW 175-633 and other large province-wide locals are extreme cases, but the trend towards larger locals exists in many unions. In some cases it is driven by a leadership belief in what Moody calls the "shallow power" (196) "magic of two-dimensional [union] density and central control of both contracts and organizing" rather than "real organization with depth in locals and the workplace" (194). In other cases the motivation is simply officials' desire for a structure that is easier and cheaper to administer.

Fortunately, many unionized workers belong to locals that hold monthly open membership meetings in locations reasonably accessible to workers and at which members are able to speak up and raise proposals that are debated and voted on. Provided that locals are allowed to make decisions about important local matters without interference from officials from higher levels of the union — CUPE, with its firm provisions for local autonomy, is the clearest case — such structures make democracy possible. However, structures alone do not produce democracy. A democratic culture that promotes the importance of membership control is also necessary. This is less common than the formal framework for democracy, and there are signs that it is weakening in parts of the union movement. For example, the B.C. Nurses' Union in recent years has:

> Almost fully made a transition from a member-driven, grassroots, bottom-up, social activist... vision of unionism to full-blown business unionism, with no internal debate, with no discussion at convention, with no discussion in the membership, just by a de facto process largely behind closed doors.[12]

Another aspect of the weakening of democratic culture is that little debate about important issues takes place in many unions and few elections for union office give members a choice between candidates with clearly different platforms.

Democratic membership control is impossible unless open debate can take place. This is missing in some locals and unions. Disagreement with a union's official leadership is often discouraged. Subtle or not-so-subtle signals can make it clear that there are negative consequences for those who disagree. In the words of a former CAW activist, members who get involved in the CAW learn "that they better shut up with the criticism or they are not going to have time out of the plant" to attend educational courses, conventions and the like. As a result, there is a lot of "self-censoring out of fear for the consequences," which is "poison" for democracy.[13] This is certainly not unique to the CAW. In many unions people who

> really come to... activism with some principles soon find out if they speak too much out about that they can't climb the ladder within their own organization, and many, not all, but many opt to climb the ladder and tow the line, as opposed to speak out and try and make a difference.[14]

This kind of signaling about the implications of dissent is often effective at quelling democratic debate. Other methods also have the same effect. In the CAW, the central leadership uses its Administration Caucus to run the union at conventions. The Administration Caucus functions somewhat like a political party in a one-party system. Delegates and staff who attend one of its meetings are expected to support its decisions during debates on the convention floor (Camfield 2007b).

In a minority of unions, officers and staff will do more to quell disagreement than sending signals about the benefits of loyalty to the incumbent leadership and the costs of dissent. The CAW officialdom is particularly heavy-handed: "They bully the shit out of people... they publicly embarrass people and they never want to speak out again. They hammer people."[15] Little wonder that it was the Canadian region of the United Auto Workers, later the CAW, that gave rise to the saying that if one wanted to rise in the union one had to be a graduate of the Bob White School of Obedience.[16] Such practices — which are certainly not unique to the CAW — stifle democracy and deter many people from becoming more involved in their unions.

When one moves above the local level to union sectoral, regional, provincial and national bodies, the degree of democracy declines precipitously. The election of officers at conventions of voting delegates, who may have been elected by local members or appointed by local executives, leaves those elected with a free hand to do as they please in between conventions (unless they do something that violates the union's constitution). At the highest levels of the union movement, contested elections are rare. It is standard practice for top officers to decide among themselves behind closed doors who will run for which position; other candidates almost never run. Carol Wall's 2005 candidacy for president of the CLC stands out as a rare example of an outsider mounting a serious challenge for a top spot (Levant 2005). Wall was not elected, but the level of support among low-level officials and rank-and-file activists (among all the CLC's affiliates, only CUPW's leadership endorsed Wall) for her independent 2005 campaign sent ripples through parts of the union officialdom. Since then, top officers have put more effort into "monitoring and controlling the membership."[17] Outside conventions — held every one to three years in most cases — there are no mechanisms for members to democratically direct those who hold executive office above the level of a local. In this respect, unions mirror one of the limitations of parliamentary democracy as it exists in most capitalist societies: the represented have no control over their elected representatives.

The Old and the Young

Related to the issue of democracy is the age of active union members. Massive job cuts in manufacturing, forest industries and other parts of the private sector applied through layoffs on the basis of seniority — "last hired, first fired" — have pushed up the average age of unionized workers in general and activists in particular. Little or no hiring in other areas of employment, especially into unionized permanent positions, has had the same effect. Workers aged forty-five to fifty-four are the most likely to be unionized, at 36.6 percent of workers in that age range in 2009, and those twenty-four and under the least, with 14.7 percent unionized (Statistics Canada 2009: 30). A recently-retired veteran activist reflects on the situation:

> Who controls the union is old people.... I think that sets a huge difference on how we approach things.... We start to talk about buyouts, we start to talk about early retirements, we start to talk about... how the senior people are going to benefit in the technological change, rather than talking about how the junior people [can] have jobs long-term with the same kind of benefits and the same kind of strong union to protect themselves that... was there twenty or thirty years ago.... I don't think the Canadian Union of Postal Workers is unique... unions are run by old people.[18]

A staffer on the East Coast echoes this, noting the "ageing demographic of the activist base" in the region.[19] This "wasn't always the case," as the retired CUPW activist observes. In the 1970s, when pro-union left-wing politics had more influence among young workers and when it was easier for youth (especially young white men) to get unionized jobs, "a lot more younger people" were involved in unions. Because of the restructuring of capitalism since then (see Chapter Six), today young people are less likely to have unionized jobs. The decline in the level of strikes has also affected the involvement of young people because the experience of striking often motivates people to become active union members. Strikes "do rejuvenate the union." After strikes more people often want "to be shop stewards, activists within that union... because strikes do empower people."[20]

In an effort to increase the involvement of younger members, many unions have created youth committees. However, as a CUPE staffer puts it, the way top union officers and staff approach young workers is often "very paternalistic and kind of instrumental."[21] It is often unclear what such committees should aim to achieve. Some try to train future officers, to "groom... younger activists" to bring them "into the apparatus."[22] More significantly, union meetings are often run in ways that are hard for members getting involved for the first time to understand. Unfamiliar terminology and dull routines can be off-putting. This makes meetings unappealing to most workers, whose time for activities beyond the demands of their jobs and households is limited. Explaining why young workers who checked out a union meeting usually did not show up again, someone who worked for Ford through his twenties said of his former union local, "the way the union meetings are structured, these guys [the officers] can do it with their eyes closed... [so a union meeting] doesn't seem like a place that is worth spending your Sunday mornings at."[23] Such ways of doing things contribute to low levels of involvement by young members in their unions. Also a factor for some young workers is resentment of seniority rules in collective agreements.[24] Many people do not understand how these rules reduce employer discrimination against longer-serving older workers and were hard-won gains in the class struggles of the 1940s.

Privilege and Oppression

No account of unions can be adequate if it ignores how the realities of privilege and oppression in society shape unions. Sexism, racism, hetero-sexism and the oppression of people with disabilities all exist in Canada and Quebec today (Naiman 2008). Consequently, all social institutions and organizations bear their stamp in one way or another, from schools to firms to governments to social service agencies. No one living in a society shot-through with oppression can be untouched by it, whether they are aware of how forms of oppression affect them or not. Thus it should be no surprise that unions — organizations of people who experience exploitation and alienation because they are part of the working class — are moulded by the patterns of oppression that exist in society. Thanks to small numbers of committed people working for social justice, education and action to combat oppression does take place within unions, as discussed earlier. This equity work has made a difference. Sexism, racism, heterosexism and the oppression of people with disabilities have been weakened within unions, but rather more in some than in others. However, as a whole, unions (like other major organizations in society) reproduce forms of oppression more than they disrupt them.

This reality is concisely summed up in the simple response of Carol Wall, who has a great deal of experience doing equity work in unions, to the question "to what extent do you actually think [unions] are anti-sexist and anti-racist organizations?": "No, no." As she observes, "If you look at the top union leadership, it is still... predominantly white males. There was a breakthrough in some of the unions with staff as racialized workers. However, that is problematic because they are controlled" by the top leadership. Even in locals where there are many workers of colour, white domination is most often still perpetuated in informal ways. These include the control exercised by white union officers and staff over which members get access to union educational programs and conferences.[25] Similar kinds of sexist and heterosexist practices "rooted in the informal culture of unions" (Haiven 2007: 97) help perpetuate the domination of unions by straight white men despite the fact that they make up only a minority of union members. For example, in 2010 there were five white women, one woman of colour and one indigenous man on the twenty-three-person National Executive Board of CUPE, whose membership is approximately 70 percent women.[26] Overall, it is fair to say that "internal union structures and processes that perpetuate male privilege have not been fundamentally challenged nor have gender equity goals that threaten existing gender and power relations been vigorously pursued" (Bentham 2007: 127). Anti-racist efforts have been even weaker. There are "beautiful policy statements but the walking has been really inadequate."[27] Action to address the oppression of people with disabilities is relatively new for most unions (Rayside and Valentine 2007). No mass organization can achieve internal equality within a society in which oppression is deeply-rooted, and so far, union efforts in this direction — important though they are — have achieved relatively little.

Varieties of Unionism

While unions are clearly many-sided organizations and every major union has its own distinguishing features, it is possible to identify a number of different varieties of unionism in Canada and Quebec. Each is a distinctive combination of what active unionists do and what they really believe their unions should try to do. Each is an approach to union activity and ideology, or a mode of union praxis (Camfield 2007b and 2008). These are: business unionism, corporate unionism, social unionism, mobilization unionism and social movement unionism. Characterizing the activity of a parent union or a local as mainly one of these does not capture every aspect of that organization, but identifies important features of union organization.

Business unionism has a narrow focus on collective bargaining for members of the union and adopts a generally cooperative approach to dealing with employers. Negotiating better wages and benefits is what really matters, though giving concessions in these and other aspects of bargaining is accepted as necessary in order to help companies or public sector employers continue to operate. Business unionism accepts capitalist society as it exists today. At most, its supporters advocate small changes in law and policy. If the union gets involved in political action, it will be only to support candidates in elections. Involvement with "the community" is limited to charity. For business unionists, unions should be run from the top down by officers and staff, with little membership involvement. This approach is common in unions across Canada and Quebec, including those in which other approaches are more influential; it is particularly strong among unionized skilled trades workers and university faculty, for example, and in the International Brotherhood of Teamsters and the Amalgamated Transit Union, to name just two unions.

Corporate unionism is Moody's term for the approach developed by some U.S.-based unions such as SEIU and UNITE HERE, which have some presence in Canada and Quebec. It is "a step beyond business unionism" that advocates highly centralized, staff-driven and even less democratic unions. It combines an energetic commitment to bring more workers under collective agreement coverage with an "almost religious attachment to partnerships with capital" and an "essentially administrative" vision (Moody 2007: 196). Its supporters are sometimes advocates of union alliances with community groups, with a view to building support for efforts to increase the number of unionized workers and raise union density.

Social unionism's main differences with business unionism are its much greater concern for social and political issues not directly related to the workplace and a more critical attitude to neoliberal policies. Its supporters generally rely on the same basic methods to achieve union goals, collective bargaining and parliamentary political action. Social unionists are often but not always non-confrontational in their dealings with employers and governments and wary of greater militancy and democratic membership control. Social unionism is common, especially in CUPE and other public sector unions and the CAW.

Least common in unions today are two alternative approaches.[28] *Mobilization unionism* involves taking a militant stance towards employers and commits unions to working for social change alongside community groups. It treats extra-parliamentary political action as important. People who practice this approach work to increase membership participation in their unions, but do not advocate a much greater level of union democracy. Today, this approach informs the activity of the TYRLC, for example. It was significant in the CAW in the second half of the 1990s, before the CAW officialdom began to shift to the right (Allen 2006).

Social movement unionism is committed to militancy and solidarity among unions and between unions and other social justice organizations in a struggle for progressive social change that involves extra-parliamentary action. Crucially, it puts democracy at the heart of unionism. Its supporters believe that unions should be run by active memberships and see democracy as key to building workers' power. Social movement unionism is practiced by small numbers of activists in CUPW and CUPE and by individuals scattered across other unions.

If we consider the actual activity of unions as a whole in Canada and Quebec as well as what officials say, we can see that the vast majority of union activity is social unionist or business unionist in character. Corporate unionism is much less present than it is in the U.S., though it is practiced in some of the Canadian locals of SEIU and UNITE HERE and by a small number of people in other unions who have been influenced by these unions. Mobilization unionism and social movement unionism were given a boost by union involvement in extra-parliamentary struggles in the years before and after the turn of the century: the Ontario Days of Action, the global justice protests of 2000–2001 and the 2002–2005 fightback against the aggressive neoliberal government of B.C. The end of these struggles and the more right-wing political climate in society since 9/11 drained away much of the support for alternative kinds of unionism. In particular, the CAW's evolution since the turn of the century has made it no longer a high-profile example of a union whose top leaders could credibly claim to be committed to a different approach than most other unions (the CAW's undemocratic culture meant that its top leaders' abandonment of mobilization unionism was loyally followed by most officials and rank-and-file activists). The changes in the CAW and the weakening of efforts for alternative kinds of unionism in general have been felt by the activists of working-class movement groups other than unions, which now deserve some attention.

Notes

1. Interview with Atlantic labour staffer, July 10, 2009.
2. This paragraph draws on Camfield 2008.
3. Interview with Karen Naylor, January 9, 2009.
4. Thanks to Brian McDougall for emphasizing this (personal communication).
5. Interview with John Humphrey, June 4, 2009. Humphrey was for many years a shopfloor USW activist and eventually president of his local. Prior to coming to Canada, he had been a union activist in Britain.
6. Interview with CUPE staffer, July 20, 2009.
7. Interview with Atlantic labour staffer, July 10, 2009.
8. Interview with Gene McGuckin, February 17, 2009. McGuckin, now retired, was a paperworker rank-and-file activist or local officer for three decades, first in the Canadian Paperworkers Union and then in the CEP.
9. Interview with Shellie Bird, May 31, 2009.
10. For example, see the accounts of USW Local 6500 in McKeigan 2008 and Mulroy 2008.
11. Information on the local drawn from <www.ufcw175.com> and an e-mail from Local 175 & 633 Membership Services to author, August 17, 2009.
12. Interview with Will Offley, February 14, 2009. Connected to this shift is the BCNU's attempt to entice Licensed Practical Nurses to leave HEU and join BCNU, which led to its suspension from the CLC (letter from Ken Georgetti, President of the CLC, to Jim Sinclair, President of the B.C. Fed, July 30, 2009).
13. Interview with Euan Gibb, June 10, 2009.
14. Interview with HEU staffer, February 16, 2009.
15. Interview with Euan Gibb, June 10, 2009.
16. White was Canadian Director of the UAW and then CAW President from 1978 to 1992. My source for the term is auto union activist Bruce Allen, who recalls first

hearing it used in jest by CAW official Peggy Nash at a party held for White when he left the presidency of the CAW to become president of the CLC (e-mail from Bruce Allen to author, August 18, 2009).

17. Anonymous interview, June 11, 2009.
18. Interview with John Friesen, November 19, 2008.
19. Interview with Atlantic labour staffer, July 10, 2009.
20. Interview with John Friesen, November 19, 2008.
21. Interview with CUPE staffer, July 20, 2009.
22. Interview with Will Offley, February 14, 2009.
23. Interview with Euan Gibb, June 10, 2009.
24. Interview with CUPE staffer, July 20, 2009.
25. Interview with Carol Wall, June 12, 2009. See also the discussion with Marie Clarke Walker and Beverley Johnson (Edelson 2009).
26. The figures for the CUPE NEB are from information at <cupe.ca>.
27. Anonymous interview, June 11, 2009.
28. Terminology here can be confusing. What I call mobilization unionism is called social movement unionism by some writers, but I believe it is a serious mistake to blur together what really are two quite different kinds of unionism (Camfield 2007b). The now-defunct Solidarity Caucus brought together some supporters of social movement unionism in B.C. — see its "Statement of Purpose" <solidaritycaucus. org>. Arguments for these two alternative approaches have been developed most clearly by U.S. activists. For the case for what I call mobilization unionism, see Fletcher and Gapasin 2008. Moody 2007 argues for social movement unionism. Downs 2009b and Early 2008 are reviews of Fletcher and Gapasin's book by supporters of social movement unionism.

4. Other Working-Class Movement Organizations

Most of this book is about unions because they make up the vast bulk of the working-class movement in Canada and Quebec, with 4.2 million members (Statistics Canada 2009), tens of thousands of whom are active unionists. Almost every year more working-class people go on strike than take part in any other kind of collective action against employers or governments.[1] Nevertheless, it would be a mistake to ignore other forms of working-class movement organization.

The "extraordinary act of defiance" of a "sixteen-day round-the-clock blockade" (Ng 2009: 164) by non-unionized immigrant workers of colour at Progressive Moulded Products of Vaughan, Ontario, to protest their employer shutting down was a rare example of public collective action by informally organized workers in the summer of 2008.[2] Informal organization among workers is often ignored precisely because it is informal. It is rarely visible to people who are not directly involved in it and is almost never studied or written about. The level of informal organization in the working class in Canada and Quebec today appears to be quite low, and what does exist is generally weak. Yet some workers do organize themselves informally against their bosses. They may engage in covert activities such as coordinated sick-ins and slow-downs. Worker-initiated union drives grow out of informal networks of people who have been "talking union." Militants in a unionized workplace may organize informally against the ratification of a concessionary tentative agreement, as in the successful "Vote No" effort at Ford's Oakville plant in 2008 (Gibb 2008), or to support a candidate for union office. Informal movement organization also happens when working-class people get together in their neighbourhoods to respond to oppression or injustice. For instance, sometimes working-class people of colour organize informally to respond to racism in schools or racist policing. The group that came together after sixteen-year-old Faraz Suleman, whose mother was a CUPE member, was shot dead by a York Regional Police detective in 1996 was an example of this (Lukas and Persad 2004: 38).

Formal working-class movement organizations other than unions also exist. In comparison with unions, they are few in number and have not many activists or members, but some of them are often in the news.

Workers' centres — the Workers' Action Centre (WAC) in Toronto (Monsebraaten 2009), the Immigrant Workers' Centre in Montreal (IWC)

(Choudry et al. 2009), the Windsor Workers' Action Centre (Ross and Drouillard 2009), Winnipeg's Workers' Organizing Resource Centre (WORC) (Bickerton and Stearns 2006) — are one kind of such organization. Workers' centres share the mission of attempting to help workers — usually non-unionized — on a "community" rather than a workplace basis. In Canada and Quebec, they have pushed at the provincial level for stronger employment standards legislation, since these laws provide crucial protection for non-unionized workers. There are important differences between the existing workers' centres. WAC staff and volunteers consciously encourage workers to organize themselves to press employers for their rights and to win changes to legislation, with the goal of building lasting self-organized workers' networks. Anti-racist feminism informs WAC's emphasis on precariously employed workers of colour.[3] WORC's efforts, on the other hand, have involved advocacy for workers denied basic employment standards rights, but without WAC's approach to organizing workers. In addition to dealing with non-unionized workers' concerns, IWC supporters have promoted union organizing by immigrant workers, assisted unionized workers who have been poorly represented by union officials and run labour education workshops.

Injured workers' groups, such as those that make up the Ontario Network of Injured Workers' Groups and similar groups in other provinces, are another kind of organization. Their focus is on the injustices experienced by people injured on the job. There are also a handful of groups of activists who work in solidarity with workers without citizenship or permanent resident status, such as Vancouver and Toronto-based Justicia for Migrant Workers, whose focus is migrant farmworkers.

A final kind of organization is activist groups that do not identify as "workers' rights" groups (and whose members may or may not think of themselves as workers),[4] but whose members are, in fact, primarily working-class people taking action on issues that affect workers. No One Is Illegal (NOII) groups in several cities and related networks like Montreal's Solidarity Across Borders, which are active around immigrant rights and in solidarity with the struggles of indigenous people and other anti-racist struggles, are examples of this kind of organization. So too are anti-poverty groups, such as OCAP in Toronto and those linked in Quebec's unemployed workers' network Mouvement autonome et solidaire des sans-emploi, which are active around issues affecting low-paid wage-earners and people on social assistance. In Quebec, tenants' groups and organizations of residents of particular lower-income neighbourhoods are more common than they are in Canada; most such associations of people that deal with housing problems and other urban issues are also part of the working-class movement.

It is obvious this is a very diverse range of small organizations. Yet many of them share an emphasis on encouraging workers to organize and take action themselves that is different from contract unionism's emphasis on people being represented by union officials. Most have little money, few or no paid staff and small memberships. They have none of the rights that unions have, but they are also free of the restrictions that labour law imposes on unions. In general, their activists also tend to be more radical and younger than union activists. Because such groups must so often take to the streets and appeal for public support in order to have any impact, they are often more visible to the population at large than unions are. In part because of how and where they organize, the outlook and culture of activists in such groups tends to be more feisty and less respectful of "official channels" than most union activists. Sometimes activists in these groups know as little about the most pressing concerns and everyday realities of union activists as most union activists know about theirs. It is not surprising, then, that relations between such groups and the union officialdom are often distant or tense.

Notes

1. Exceptions include unusual years like 1996, when the Days of Action in several Ontario cities involved more than the 276,000 workers who were involved in a labour dispute that year, and 2003, when the very low number of strikers, 79,000, was well below the number of people who took to the streets in Quebec and Canada to protest the U.S. assault on Iraq. Figures on strikers are from Statistics Canada 2009.
2. Union organizing efforts by CAW and USW had earlier failed at PMP (anonymous interview, June 11, 2009).
3. Interview with workers' rights activist, June 5, 2009.
4. For example, a supporter of No One Is Illegal-Vancouver states that people in that group "consider themselves part of the community struggle, which encompasses various levels" (interview, February 14, 2009).

5. Assessing the Contemporary Working-Class Movement

It is now time to make an overall assessment of the movement in Canada and Quebec today. Most discussions of this topic focus on union density and membership figures. It is true that the absolute number of unionized workers has not been shrinking while union density has been declining very slowly. This stands in contrast to the U.S., where the absolute number of members has been falling since 1980 and the density rate has been falling since 1953. Today it is only half of what it was in 1980 (Moody 2007: 100). It is also true that union institutions remain generally stable, though some parent unions have lost large numbers of members and therefore income (for example, job losses reduced the CAW's membership from 265,000 in 2005 to 225,000 in 2009, with most of the drop in 2008–2009 [CAW 2009]). This relative stability has contributed to complacency in some quarters about the state of unions. But union membership and density statistics only tell us something about the movement's size. Size is only one of its features, and size does not translate directly into power. For example, the percentage of wage-earners in France who are union members is much lower than in Canada and Quebec (but collective agreement coverage is much higher), yet the working-class movement in France is definitely stronger.[1]

The Contradictions of Unions

In assessing the unions that make up the bulk of the movement, it is important to recognize that unions are *contradictory* for the working class. When we look at history, we can see that unions globally have been organizations created by workers to defend themselves within the confines of capitalism, a social order in which the profits and power of capital trump human needs.[2] Unions vary enormously, but all unions are contradictory because they both *reproduce* features of capitalist society and *resist* aspects of it. Features of capitalism are imprinted on unions. We can see this in how unions reflect the divisions among workers along gender and racial lines and the division between wage-earners and unwaged workers. Unions are shaped by how wage-workers are subordinated to bosses and divided hierarchically into groupings with different levels of pay, status and control on the job. Some unions are much more geared to resistance than others — more militant in their opposition to employers and governments, less timid in their goals, broader in their solidarity, more democratic.

The extent to which unionized workers attempt to develop some kind of political challenge to the power of capitalists varies widely. All unions must negotiate with employers about wages and working conditions and engage in day-to-day skirmishes about how management exercises its power over workers on the job. This is true for even the most active, combative and democratic unions with leaders and many members who are deeply committed to a long-term strategy for radical social change. Even such unions must reckon with the constraints imposed on them by the competitive environment in which private sector employers operate or by funding limits in the public sector, both of which are beyond the control of even the strongest single union.

Another complicating factor is that once unions establish stable collective bargaining relations with employers, they tend to acquire more full-time officers and staff. Such officials live a different existence than the workers they represent. The more that being a full-time official becomes a job rather than a temporary commitment, the more it fosters a different world view. Full-time officials depend on the security of the union as an institution; without it, they could not be full-time officials. This is true no matter what kind of unionism an official believes in. As a result, full-time officials tend to treat the preservation of the union institution as an end in itself, independently of what the union means for workers. They also tend to favour ways of conducting union work that give them more say, at the expense of democratic membership control over the union (Camfield 2009b).

To the extent that unions are democratic, they are organizations through which people can act collectively as workers to defend themselves, try to improve their pay and working conditions and take action on issues that transcend their own particular workplaces. Whether members actually do so at a given time is another matter; the point is that they *could*. When workers are simply *unable* to democratically act together through their unions, unions are not workers' organizations, but organizations run by a labour officialdom on behalf of workers or in its own self-interest. In some circumstances, such unions can be reformed and made democratic. In other cases, the grip of the officialdom is so strong that democratization is impossible (such organizations are not working-class movement organizations of any kind).

Union locals beyond hope of democratic reform are extreme cases of a phenomenon that is widespread in unions (and many other organizations and institutions in contemporary capitalist society): bureaucracy. This term is often used to refer to government departments, other complex formal structures or the layer of full-time union officers and staff that is referred to in this book as the union officialdom. In this book, the concept of bureaucracy is used in a different, specific sense: it exists where people are subject to formal rules that limit their ability to determine what they do and how they do it, rules they cannot easily change. In unions, bureaucracy exists through the rules found in collective agreements, imposed by labour law and enshrined in union constitutions (Camfield 2009b).

The Working-Class Movement in Canada and Quebec

Turning now to workers' organizations as they exist in Canada and Quebec today, what do we find? At the most basic level, unions today give workers a legally-recognized way to organize collectively and negotiate with their employers. This makes unionization an alternative to having to deal with employers as isolated individuals. This makes a difference for wage-earners: "What force on earth is weaker than the feeble strength of one?" asks the labour song "Solidarity Forever." For people covered by one, a collective agreement takes labour out of competition: it limits the ability of an employer to push workers to outbid each other in a downward spiral of falling wages and worsening working conditions.

However, unions in Canada and Quebec only organize workers collectively in fragmented ways. The breadth of collective organization is limited by the way the state divides unionized workers into thousands of bargaining units that are usually narrow in scope. At times, unionized workers are able to unite across bargaining unit lines, especially when they all work for the same employer. In rare circumstances, unionized workers come together on a wider basis, as in the strikes by other workers to support health care workers and teachers in B.C. in 2004 and 2005 (Camfield 2006, 2009a). Almost never do unions mobilize workers on a class-wide basis, drawing non-unionized workers and union members together in common action. Most often, as we have seen, unionized workers act in very restricted ways, using the collective bargaining and grievance and arbitration procedures of contract unionism. All this is the result of the highly bureaucratic framework imposed on unions by labour law ever since the 1940s. Other workers' movement organizations are not constrained by labour law. Often more dynamic, militant and radical than most unions, their members are sometimes capable of organizing street actions that involve hundreds or even thousands of people. Yet these groups, which have their own weaknesses, are too few and too small to have an impact on the disunity of the working class on a mass scale.

While it makes a difference whether a union practices business, corporate, social, mobilization or social movement unionism, all unionism today is contract unionism. The state, through labour law, dictates that unions are organizations centred on bargaining units and structured around collective agreements and the grievance and arbitration system through which contracts are administered. The state also enlists union officials in upholding the law and disciplining workers covered by their contracts. The union officialdom is guaranteed the smooth flow of union dues collected by employers from all bargaining unit members in exchange for keeping unions "responsible" organizations that do not challenge management's control of the workplace or capitalism itself.

Contract unionism has never been as unchallenged within the working-class movement as it is today. The wave of wildcat strikes, defiance of anti-union court injunctions and the radicalization of much of the movement in Quebec of the 1960s and early 1970s (Palmer 2009; Mills 2010) are not even distant memories for most of today's workers. Traditions of militancy and radicalism have been greatly weakened. Mid-contract strikes against employers, sympathy strikes and political strikes are all but extinct (the sympathy strikes in B.C. in 2004-2005 stand out as exceptional). Workplace direct action of all kinds is at an extremely low level. This is not merely a short-term response to the economic crisis that hit in 2008. The annual number of mid-contract strikes fell sharply after the recession of the early 1980s and dropped to lower levels after the recession of the early 1990s. But the twenty-seven reported between 2004 and 2008 (years that saw very low official unemployment levels before the onset of the crisis) was much fewer than the ninety-eight recorded over the previous five years.[3] The neoliberal assault that has led to the decline in legal strikes has had an even greater impact on workers' willingness to strike outside the law. Following the inability of the Ontario Days of Action (Camfield 2000) and very large protests in B.C. and Quebec to stop attacks by right-wing governments, support for extra-parliamentary political action has also shrunk. "The movement has turned more inward, so lobbying becomes the actions," is how one person has described it.[4] As this has happened, divisions between the union officialdom and social justice activists outside the unions have deepened.[5]

Even within the framework of contract unionism, we have seen a decline in the union officialdom's willingness to resist. The officialdom today is often quite preoccupied with the defence of unions as institutions. An HEU staffer observes:

> I think there's just a real lack of solidarity, and any real focus on representing workers and the working class, as opposed to how do we get through this and survive. So I see a lot of the survival of the union, the institution is at the top of people's minds instead of workers' rights being advanced.... It seems that sometimes the survival of the institution is farther up the priority than it should be.[6]

This preoccupation can lead union officials to try to ensure workers do not resist employer demands or otherwise act in ways that could lead to struggles that risk harming union institutions or bargaining relationships. A prime example is the way HEU's 2004 strike, discussed in Chapter One, was brought to an abrupt end. More often, union officials act proactively to prevent confrontations from taking place. This is captured by a former CAW staffer's description of the CAW officialdom's current role: "To actually make sure that there is no fight back and make sure that people are sufficiently scared and ha[ve] sufficient faith in them that they wo[n't] do very much."[7]

When union officials behave in this way and get what they want, organizations of workers' self-defence become obstacles to workers defending themselves. This is not a brand new development. In fact, it amplifies the role that union officials have so often played since the 1940s, when labour laws enlisted them in policing the workplace to prevent wildcat strikes and "obey now, grieve later" became the rule. Today, the tendency for union officials to act to deter workers' resistance is fueled by the growing acceptance of concessions in both public and private sector unions. The officialdom's acceptance of concessions as supposedly inevitable (as opposed to believing that concessions are repugnant but sometimes forced on workers) has a significant impact: "When unions accept the *legitimacy* of giving back previously-won wage, benefit, or working conditions gains in the name of competitiveness or productivity, it signifies a fundamental shift in the terms of class struggle" (Brennan 2005). "Workers did not form unions to go backwards" but "to defend their dignity, to defend what they have and to move forwards whenever possible" (Allen 2009b). The appeal of unions to workers can only fall when unions come to be associated with giving concessions to employers without a struggle.

Officials who are concerned about getting workers to accept give-backs are likely to undermine union democracy. Most local unions are at least somewhat subject to the democratic control of their members. Some more bureaucratic locals could be democratized if a culture of democracy developed among enough members and led to action for democratic reform. Others, such as mega-locals, are beyond hope of democratization. Across unions, however, the belief that important organizations in society should be run by "experts" rather than by ordinary people influences how members and staff think and act. This continues to be a strong tradition in unions. This can be seen in the bureaucratic features of most union constitutions and local union bylaws and in substitutionist behaviour by active members as well as staff. Overall, the level of union democracy has suffered in recent years as a result of concession-selling officials asserting their control. The influence of corporate unionism, with its vision of larger staff-driven locals as the best response to large and powerful firms, has also been anti-democratic.

Members who are deprived of control over their unions cannot develop the activist and leadership abilities that some workers do gain from the experience of democratically running their own local union affairs. Across unions, the skills that workers are most likely to acquire are related to filing grievances and becoming familiar with contracts and laws. This is true where social unionism prevails as well as where business unionism is the norm. Less often, the experience of an organizing drive, a strike or a community-based campaign allows workers to develop activist skills. Small numbers of workers discover new ways of understanding workplace and "big picture" issues in contemporary society through union education. A lot of informal as well as formal learning happens in unions. But what is learned today most often has to do with the central activities of a timid contract unionism that treats concessions as legitimate. This kind of learning does not help workers to organize themselves to resist the actions of employers and governments or to change their unions.

The culture in most unions today is, as argued earlier, one that encourages members who become involved not to challenge what officials do and say. Many activists discover that asking tough questions or demonstrating a commitment to principles of democracy and solidarity means they will not be selected to attend education courses or other union activities that involve paid time off work. Instead, they may be labeled as troublemakers for whom members should not vote in union elections.[8] This is not a new experience, but the climate of conformity has grown stronger. Principled action and vigorous disagreement with the positions taken by leading officials has become less common. Even active unionists rarely encounter dissenting perspectives. In this environment, critical thinking and democracy suffer while opportunism and careerism can thrive more easily.

All this affects political action. Union political action, when it happens today, is usually about campaigning for those politicians seen as "the least bad." This rock-bottom standard mirrors the low hopes that most workers have for what unions can try to accomplish through collective bargaining; both are evidence of how working-class expectations have been lowered over three decades of attacks by business and government. Today, political action often means more or less uncritically backing parties and candidates supported by capitalists. When it does, political action actually undermines the independence of workers from the ruling class on which the working-class movement depends. Union political action today is rarely about trying to develop the working class as a force to change society in the way that supporters of mobilization and social movement unionism and many workers' centre activists believe is necessary.

When we look beyond individual unions to unions as a whole, there is little unity to be seen. The officialdom of each union generally acts in what it sees as its own interests rather than the interests of unionized workers or the working class as a whole. As a CUPE local officer has written,

> The union movement is not much of a movement, these days, but a collection of individual unions pre-occupied with servicing the membership they have and competing with other unions for new members.... Many unions in the same sector, provincial federation or labour council do not even have a minimal working relationship with one another. (Kidd 2005: 30)

An insider describes the competition between unions in this way: "We f[ight] with each other, we raid each other because it is more convenient, a faster way to enhance our own membership base, without knowing we are chasing after our own tails."[9] The 2009 split in UNITE HERE (created as a merger of UNITE and HERE in 2004) that created the SEIU-affiliated Workers United and a divisive fight over representation rights and assets is but a recent example of "self-destructive internecine conflict" that has hurt workers (Hickey 2009). The number of activists involved in CLC labour councils, which bring local activists from CLC-affiliated unions in a city or region together, has declined, with some notable exceptions. Some labour councils have been folded or become inactive.[10]

To sum up, then, the working-class movement is almost entirely made up of unions. Unionization today generally provides at least some degree of protection from the power of employers. For workers, contract unionism makes union membership more about representation by someone else than it is about self-organization. Nevertheless, unionization does allow workers to deal with employers collectively rather than as lone individuals. Most locals are run by small numbers of people, often in substitutionist ways. "The notion that 'we are the union' only rings true in a few activist-based unions."[11] Nevertheless, unionization is the only legally-sanctioned way that people can organize in their own self-defence in the places where they work for wages. How unionized workers resist their employers is, however, tightly restricted by law and often by the union officialdom. Union officials are often preoccupied with preserving the union institution (in the last instance, its funds, property and the representation rights that generate dues income) and their bargaining relationships with employers. The ability of workers to use union organization to defend themselves is put to the test when it seems possible that workers might fight back in ways that are not approved by officials. Most unions do not function consistently as obstacles to workers defending their immediate interests. However, the growing acceptance of concessions in the officialdom is increasingly leading officials to try to block workers' resistance or prevent workers from taking steps to resist employer demands in the first place.

Still, local unions are often at least somewhat democratic organizations despite the sway officials often exert and the bureaucratic ways in which unions are so often structured. The barriers posed by systemic racism, sexism, heterosexism and the oppression of people with disabilities and the difficulties often faced by younger union members also reduce the level of union democracy and influence union decisions and priorities in negative ways. Belonging to a parent union makes unionized workers part of an organization of workers beyond their own workplace. That said, links between members who belong to different locals of the same union are usually weak at best. Links between members of different unions — through labour council, for example — are often even weaker.

What does unionization mean today for the organization of the working class as a force in society? To the extent that being covered by collective agreements reduces competition among wage-earners — for example, by curbing management favouritism and self-serving behaviour by individuals at the expense of their coworkers — it fosters a sense of common cause. This sustains the most elementary level of workers' solidarity. But the fragmented structure of collective bargaining does not unite workers on a class-wide basis. Contract unionism's built-in emphasis on workers being represented by union officials (rather than workers' self-organization) encourages workers to be passive. Most of the skills and knowledge learned by people who become active in their unions is related to bureaucratic contract unionism and does not develop collective capacities to understand or resist the attacks to which people are being subjected in capitalist society today. Worse, concession bargaining and supporting candidates for elected office who do not oppose neoliberalism only reinforces workers' subordination and low expectations. Such activities cannot strengthen the working class as a social force. Worst of all, stifling resistance, raiding, negotiating contract provisions that divide workers (such as two-tier wages and benefits) and weakening union democracy actually corrode workers' unity and ability to engage in collective action. This contributes to weakening the working class as a force in society. In contrast, strikes that do not end in defeats for workers, organizing drives and other kinds of workers' collective action do foster solidarity, self-organization and the belief that it is possible for people to act together and have an impact. These experiences have not disappeared despite the hard times for labour. Small numbers of members in a few unions are fortunate to have access to labour education programs that really do open their eyes about how capitalism works and equip them to be more effective activists. An overall assessment cannot be straightforward: unions today have important effects on the shaping of the working class as a social force, but these effects are limited and contradictory.

The Movement and the Rest of the Working Class

An analysis of the movement must also look at where it fits in relation to the working class as a whole. As we have seen, union ideology rarely thinks of unions this way, as the unionized minority of the working class. Instead, workers outside the unions are usually seen as part of "the community" — perhaps worthy of charity or an organizing drive, but not potential allies in a common working-class struggle. One symptom of how the union officialdom does not act as if it is responsible to fight for all workers is the low priority given to defending and improving employment standards laws, which provide non-union workers with most of the weak workplace rights they have, and social assistance, the last fall-back for the jobless. A case in point was the response to the legislated weakening of employment standards in Ontario in 2001. Active opposition was led by the Employment Standards Working Group, a very small group of social justice activists (some of whom went on to form the WAC discussed in the last chapter). The level of involvement by union officials and rank-and-file members was "dismal." As a result, a government move that disproportionately affected low-paid women workers and workers of colour met with little resistance (Hammond 2001).

A conservative focus on defending current members or the union as an institution also has the effect of reproducing forms of oppression within the working class: "Under pressure to save jobs and protect incumbent union members from closures and restructuring, many unions resort to defending the status quo to the disadvantage of groups such as racialized minorities and women" (Yates 2007: 66). At best, this amounts to a short-term defense of one section of the working class that does nothing to help other workers. But defending the inequitable status quo often seems to union officials and activists like the best they can do given anti-union moves by employers and governments and a low level of mobilization among unionized workers. Yet simply defending the status quo leaves workers divided and is self-defeating for unions. When union leaders act in this way, they reinforce "the view of unions as institutions of privilege with little or no commitment to substantive change in the labour market or workplace" (66). In the eyes of many, as the CAW's top economist admits, "unions have come to be seen as promoting the special interests of unionized workers, rather than fighting for the interests of ALL workers" (Stanford 2009).

This perception has some real basis in fact. Contract unionism narrows the vision of unions in general, but unions that practice business unionism in particular have gained a well-deserved reputation of only being interested in their own members. Because union membership is disproportionately white, focusing on only the interests of the existing membership distances unions from the growing numbers of workers of colour. The relatively little effort unions are putting into reaching out to non-unionized workers and organizing the unorganized also feeds the perception that unions fight only for their own members. Another aspect of the narrowness of unions is how over the decades since the 1940s, much more of their efforts have gone into winning pensions, drug coverage, dental insurance and other health benefits for workers covered by their collective agreements than into the harder challenge of achieving better public pensions and health care for all. As a result, unionized workers now find themselves defending what some call a "private welfare state" rather than programs and rights available to all wage-earners. The 2009 Toronto municipal workers' strike illuminated this clearly. Yet another reason for the view that unions are "institutions of privilege" is the reality of systemic sexism, racism and other forms of oppression in unions. For example,

> Many indigenous people continue to maintain an ambivalent view of organized labour because unions have not always served the immediate interests of their communities. This has especially been the case in the resource extraction industry, which often pits the rights of non-native workers against indigenous nations whose lands continue to be stolen for capitalist development. (Pitawanakwat 2006: 33)

Unions have not always served the interests of non-indigenous workers of colour and women, either. One way in which this has been true is the low priority given to fighting for contract provisions and laws that challenge racist and sexist bias in who employers hire (employment equity).

Union sexism and racism in the past and, to a lesser extent, the present have given many people reasons to dislike or distrust the main organizations of the working-class movement. The narrow focus and limited power of contract unionism to resist employer tyranny in the workplace has hurt the reputation of unions among workers. Inadequate internal democracy and officials who put little effort into fighting even for the members of the unions they head have had the same effect. The barrage of anti-union messages in the media gets more of a hearing because of negative features of unions today. As a result, many non-unionized workers are not drawn to unions, though many still do wish for union protection (Jackson 2005: 182). This can only delight employers, who always benefit when wage-earners are unorganized and the working class divided.

Decay in the Movement

It matters that the total number of unionized workers in Canada and Quebec is not falling and that union density is declining only slowly. Wage settlements and other outcomes of collective agreements also matter. But studies that only examine such things miss more than they illuminate about the working-class movement today. The first part of this book has looked at what kind of organizations unions and other workers' movement groups actually are today, at what people do through them and how this matters for people who must rely on working for wages. These organizations are extremely important for the working class. They are all that wage-workers and the unwaged have to defend themselves against capitalists and governments whose determination to expand corporate profits and power has never been greater. These are also the only existing organizations that give workers any possibility of changing society in ways that reflect their needs and interests.

Looked at in this light, the movement as it exists today is both *necessary* and *profoundly inadequate* for the working class. In many ways, this was just as true during the second half of the twentieth century as it is today.[12] But, as we have seen, there are also signs that unions are evolving in ways that make it somewhat harder for workers to use them as organizations through which they can act collectively in their own interests than was the case in the second half of the twentieth century. The other organizations of the movement are too few and small to have much of an impact.

Most of the labour officialdom is resigned to putting up little or no serious resistance to demands for concessions. Many top union officers and staff are also willing to try to stop those who do want to resist from interfering with their concessionary dealings. Union democracy in the second half of the twentieth century was, for the most part, much weaker than what supporters of rank-and-file control were able to achieve in the most democratic parts of the movement. But today, the erosion in some unions of democracy, and the culture and basic structures that make it possible, means more union-ized workers find themselves unable to be part of decision-making in their locals. The significant under-representation of people of colour in unions at a time when the percentage of wage-earners in Canada and Quebec that is affected by racism is larger than ever before and growing has created a greater distance between unions and the non-unionized working class. The decline of the union presence in the private sector, where most wage-earners are employed, has done the same thing. The dominance of older members has created a greater distance between many other workers and their unions. Political action in support of politicians tied to business and parties that do not oppose neoliberalism ties unions more closely to the ruling class than was the case when many unions supported the NDP and the NDP was independent of capital (even though its politics were never anti-capitalist). Taken together, these changes amount to a process of *the decay of unions as working-class movement organizations*.

When unionism was reorganized in the 1940s in bureaucratic ways that tightly restricted what workers could do through unions, unions in Canada and Quebec became something other than simply working-class movement organizations. They also became legally-sanctioned institutions through which the state regulates relations between some wage-earners and their employers in ways that limit working-class power. Today, unions remain stable as labour relations institutions. For the most part, they remain working-class movement organizations of a particular kind. But in general, unions are becoming more removed from the working class than they were through the second half of the twentieth century. This process of decay is uneven within parent unions and between them. Even many locals dominated by corrupt and conservative full-time officials could be made into democratic organizations by membership revolts. But when workers are less able to defend their interests through unions and less likely to imagine doing so, this, in turn, makes it less likely that workers will claim or reclaim unions as their own organizations. How the working-class movement came to be in such a state is the question we will explore in the next chapter.

Notes

1. For an introduction to unions in France, see Jeffreys 2000. For data on collective agreement coverage and union density in France, see <worker-participation.eu>.
2. For an excellent introduction to the history of working-class movements, see Mason 2008.
3. Unpublished data provided by the Strategic Policy, Analysis and Workplace Information Directorate of Human Resources and Skills Development Canada.
4. Anonymous interview, June 11, 2009.
5. This was visible during and after the protests against the G-20 summit in Toronto in June 2010. "There were some union statements that condemned police actions and mass arrests in the wake of the demonstrations. A number of unions, including the CLC, denounced the repressive bail conditions handed some of those accused of conspiracy, but, with some exceptions, union officials have not gone out of their way to give much financial and political support for those still languishing in jail or mounting expensive legal defences" (e-mail from Herman Rosenfeld to author, December 21, 2010).
6. Interview with HEU staffer, February 16, 2009.
7. Interview with Herman Rosenfeld, June 7, 2009. Rosenfeld was an auto worker union activist for many years and later a CAW staffer.
8. This is a familiar experience for many union activists I have known. McKeigan 2008 and Mulroy 2008 are two published accounts.
9. Anonymous interview, June 11, 2009.
10. Interview with Atlantic labour staffer, July 10, 2009.
11. Anonymous interview, June 11, 2009.
12. See, for example, Palmer 1992 (268–416).

6. The Roots of Today's Problems

As a mass movement with many thousands of active members in organizations whose formal membership numbers in the millions, the shape of today's working-class movement is the result of numerous forces acting over time. The interwoven social relations — including class, gender, race and nation — that structure paid work, households and community life in Canada and Quebec have all structured the movement to some extent. It is impossible to discuss all of these, so this chapter focuses on five key developments and forces that have been important in making the working-class movement what it is today: the transformation of unionism in the 1940s, the loss since the 1950s of much of the infrastructure that fosters workers' capacity for collective action, the neoliberal restructuring of capitalism since the late 1970s, the decline of the left over the same period and the direction charted by the top union officials who have the most power within the movement. These have decisively put their stamp on the contemporary movement and contributed to the decay that has been taking place. Understanding these developments and forces is particularly important for people who would like to see the movement change course and head in a different direction.

The Transformation of Unionism[1]

It is impossible to understand why the working-class movement in the early twenty-first century is the way it is without understanding how the movement was changed by what happened in the 1940s. Events of that decade have had long-term effects on the movement that were foreseen by very few, if any, of the people who participated in the turbulent struggles of the time.

During and after the Second World War, tens of thousands of workers in manufacturing, mining, forestry, shipping and other sectors — mostly less-skilled men who had no place in the existing craft unions of skilled workers — defied wartime restrictions on strikes by walking off the job. The number of union members leaped to more than twice the pre-war level. This wave of strikes and union organizing was fueled by workers' desire to raise wages and improve conditions on the job by curbing the unrestricted power of supervisors and managers under which they suffered. Workers' action won important gains, including better pay and limits on arbitrary management power.

In response to the wartime strikes, in 1944 the federal government brought in new rights for unions that were linked with new restrictions (elements of this new regime, such as grievance procedures and management's rights clauses, had been appearing in some collective agreements before 1944). After the end of the war, these rights and restrictions were entrenched in federal and provincial labour laws, where they remain to this day. Workers who wanted to bargain collectively with their employer now needed to apply to a labour board for certification under the law. Employers were compelled to bargain with a certified union, but workers who were not members of a certified bargaining unit were prohibited from striking. Labour board rulings determined who belonged to a bargaining unit, and units were usually defined narrowly (for example, by putting mostly male production workers and mostly female office workers employed by the same firm into different units). Every contract now had to include a grievance and arbitration procedure to resolve disputes that arose while it was in effect as well as a management's rights clause recognizing that the employer's power over workplace and business decisions was unrestricted except where specifically limited by the contract. A strike by unionized workers was allowed only after the expiry of their collective agreements and after going through a conciliation process. Workers could legally strike only as part of bargaining for their own contract, and not over disputes that arose during a contract, in solidarity with other workers, to support a political demand on the government or to pressure the employer to recognize their union. Union officials were required to ensure that bargaining unit members did not take illegal strike action. It is clear that the governments that adopted this new regime of labour law wanted to ensure that if employers were to be required to bargain with unions where workers wanted to be unionized then the power of unionized workers would be severely limited. This regime made unions into more than the main organizations of the working-class movement. They also became institutions through which the relationship between unionized wage-workers and employers was regulated by the state.

At the same time as the new wartime rights and restrictions were being written into post-war legislation, vicious political conflict was taking place within unions. After the Cold War between the states aligned with the U.S. and those aligned with the U.S.S.R. began in 1946, political conflict intensified in the unions between officials who supported the social democratic Cooperative Commonwealth Federation (CCF — ancestor of the NDP) and the sizeable current in the unions led by Communists (at the time, the Communist Party of Canada [CPC] existed under the name Labour-Progressive Party). CCF backers took advantage of the anti-communist frenzy being whipped up by politicians, the press and church leaders to smash their political opponents in the unions. Between 1947 and 1950, most Communists and other leftists tagged as "reds" were forced from union office. They included non-Communists who resisted the purge, among them a Sudbury mine unionist elected as a CCF MPP. In the course of the purge, red-baiting and intimidation were common. Unions that the anti-communist purgers could not take over were expelled from the two main union centrals of the day, the Canadian Congress of Labour and the Trades and Labour Congress (which merged in 1956 to form the CLC). Expelled unions were then raided by other unions, often with employer support. Labour boards decertified a number of Communist-led locals and, in 1950, the entire Canadian Seamen's Union (whose members had also been targeted by armed gangsters hired by the leader of the union engaged in raiding them). By the time the dust settled at the end of the decade, the Communist-led current in the unions had been decisively defeated and dispersed. Whatever their failings (and there were many), Communists in the unions had been critics of capitalism who supported extra-parliamentary action by labour. The purge drove such ideas to the margins of the workers' movement.

Unions changed as a result of the combination of the new regime of labour law and the anti-communist purge. Champions of the changes were happy to describe this as "responsible" unionism. By this they meant an approach that fully endorsed capitalism, accepted that unionism would be defined by the negotiation and administration of binding contracts that prohibited mid-contract strikes and sought political change only through established constitutional channels — lobbying and the ballot box. Such unionism had long been supported by some in the working-class movement, but vigorously opposed by many; now it reigned supreme. Unionists who adopted this approach rejected the very methods of collective action — above all, strikes in defiance of unjust laws and regulations — that had won new rights for unions during the war.

Having union officials systematically keep members in line on behalf of employers and the state changed the relationship between workers and unions. Some officials had certainly acted in this way in the past, believing this would help preserve their unions in the face of hostile capitalists and governments. But now the union officialdom as a whole was required to police contracts. "Responsible" unionism also gave union activism a narrower outlook. It accepted the law's new insistence that unions were to act only on behalf of the members of the many separate bargaining units into which unionized workers were now divided and not engage in sympathy strikes. This undercut solidarity among workers in the same industry and region and across the working class as a whole. Reliance on grievances and arbitration instead of direct action built "a legalistic leadership."[2] "Responsible" unionism was much more bureaucratic than unions had been before. Laws and collective agreements added many more formal rules that limited what unionized workers could do and how they could do it to those found in union constitutions and local union by-laws. This weakened the democratic control of unions by their members. So, too, did the growing role of full-time officials who tended to see it as their job to run the unions, with the rank-and-file playing little or no role. This was due to the fact that unions became more top-heavy as more staff and full-time officer positions were created to deal with grievances and arbitration cases and negotiate increasingly complex contracts. Union democracy also suffered as a result of the Cold War anti-communist campaign, in which democratically-elected officials were driven from their posts. The anti-communist drive created a climate in the unions in which people who asked probing questions about the policies of governments or unions on domestic or international issues could be dismissed as "commies." The result was a union culture of conformity rather than discussion and debate. In addition, by explicitly recognizing management's right to run the workplace, this kind of unionism unwittingly created obstacles to future union action against systemic sexism and racism on the job.

One other important development in the 1940s that changed unions was the Rand Formula. Named after the judge who wrote the arbitration ruling to settle the bitter 1945 auto workers' strike against Ford in Windsor, the Rand Formula required all members of a bargaining unit to pay union dues, since they all benefitted from the collective agreement negotiated by union officials on their behalf. But it did not require them to join the union. Dues would be paid by "check off" — the employer would deduct them from workers' paycheques and transfer the money to the union. In exchange, union officials were required to disown wildcat strikes and discipline workers who took part in them. If they failed to do this, the company could withhold dues. This gave officials a strong incentive to oppose direct action by workers during the life of a contract. The check off not only got rid of the time-consuming task of collecting dues in the workplace; it also guaranteed that union dues would flow regardless of how workers felt about what union officials were doing. This further separated union officials from the membership. Over time, the Rand Formula spread to many other collective agreements and was incorporated into labour laws. It has been a factor in preserving unions as stable institutions and maintaining union membership numbers into the early twenty-first century.

The major expansion of unions in the public sector in the 1960s and 1970s mostly took place within the framework of "responsible" unionism; CUPW, with its origins in trail-blazing strike action by non-unionized postal workers, was an exception. In those decades, workers' militancy and radicalism challenged "responsible" unionism in parts of the movement, especially in Quebec, but did not produce an enduring alternative to it.[3] Still, unions have changed in many significant ways since the 1940s. For example, the majority of members are now women and work in the public sector, while in the 1940s, members were overwhelmingly male and mostly employed by private sector firms in manufacturing, resource extraction and transportation. Some unions now bargain for demands unheard of in the 1940s, including pay equity and protection from harassment in the workplace. More than two decades after the fall of the U.S.S.R. and the Stalinist states of Eastern Europe, Cold War anti-communism no longer influences union life. Yet unions today continue to be moulded by the same combination of law and contract that dictates so many aspects of what unionized workers are allowed to do. These forces, plus unions' own constitutions, still make unions highly bureaucratic organizations whose main activities are negotiating and administering complex binding contracts. Criticism of capitalism for its negative effects on people and the rest of nature may be occasionally heard in some unions, but full-fledged opposition to the capitalist system itself is rare. Grievances, strikes over bargaining issues, lobbying and electoral politics are still the ways in which most unions act most of the time. Few unionists advocate direct action in the workplace or the streets, sympathy strikes or political strikes. Unionism in the twenty-first century is still largely the "responsible" variety that became the norm in the working-class movement in the 1940s.

The Crumbling of the Infrastructure of Dissent

As they have developed around the world, working-class movements have always been fueled by the many ways that people have come to understand the subordinate position of workers in capitalist society from viewpoints that are critical of their subordination. Just as important are the many ways that people learn how to organize themselves to try to change unjust conditions.

A useful way of thinking about these crucial sources of energy for working-class movements is the concept of the *infrastructure of dissent*: "the means of analysis, communication, organization and sustenance that nurture the capacity for collective action" (Sears 2005: 32). The crumbling of the infrastructure of dissent is one reason why the working-class movement in Canada and Quebec is in its current condition.

From the mid-1800s to the mid-1900s, the working-class movement in Canada and Quebec arose and took different forms, including craft unions; the Knights of Labour; industrial unions infused with a militant, radical and democratic spirit; unions tied to the Roman Catholic Church; women's labour groups; industrial unions with a bureaucratic and "responsible" cast; groups of militants within unions; organizations of the unemployed; associations of immigrant workers; left-wing parties and groups committed to reforms within capitalist society; and others that sought the replacement of capitalism with socialism (Heron 1996; Palmer 1992). The many people who created and built these workers' organizations in the face of great adversity were equipped to do so by what they learned in the infrastructures of dissent.

These infrastructures were made up of many elements. There were formal and informal groups of union activists who came together around their shared visions of unionism. For instance, in Local 1005 of the Steelworkers, the union of Hamilton's Stelco workers, there were rival caucuses led by CCF and CPC members, followed in the 1960s by the Right Wing, Left Wing and Autonomy groups (Freeman 1982). Radical left-wing organizations rooted in the working class were another element. Many workers gained at least a rudimentary analysis of history, the capitalist economy and how to fight for a better world from talking with socialist fellow workers, attending political meetings and reading radical publications, whether or not they joined or remained members of a party. In some communities, radical left political organizations had mass influence. For example, the Crowsnest Pass region straddling the B.C.-Alberta border was

> a stronghold for the Socialist Party of Canada and its left wing, whose local militants went over to the CPC [Communist Party of Canada] in their majority in the early 1920s. This gave Communists a long-standing purchase on support and loyalty within the area that was not available to the CCF, which was not founded until 1932. (Langford and Frazer 2002: 49–50)

Radical political organizations did not have this much influence in most working-class communities, but they had a presence in many.

Places that allowed people to cultivate bonds based in the shared hardships and pleasures of working-class life were another dimension of local infrastructures of dissent. In Windsor, the Ukrainian Labour Farmer Temple on Drouillard Road "among other things, served as a meeting place for people trying to unionize Ford" (Sears 2005: 32). This was just one of many working-class movement halls, often set up by immigrants excluded from the dominant Anglo-Celtic culture of pre-1950 Canada. Some bars and taverns played a similar role as these movement institutions. For example, in the late nineteenth century and well into the twentieth, the Palace Hotel and Tavern in the Parkdale neighbourhood of Toronto was a site where many male unionists from the area's various factories and other workplaces met up for "socializing and political discussion" in an "atmosphere... formed by a fierce independence" (Sobel and Meurer 1994: 21). Beyond specific establishments, certain areas where many people were active in the working-class movement were places that sustained the capacity for collective action. These included the Spadina neighbourhood in Toronto, Drouillard Road in Windsor, Winnipeg's North End and the small towns of the Crowsnest Pass (Sears 2005; Silver 2010; Norton and Langford 2002).

What Alan Sears writes about the Drouillard Road area of Windsor in the 1930s and 1940s could also be said about many other areas where the working-class movement was dynamic:

> The infrastructure of dissent… developed a community of activists, with many who could think their own way through strategic and tactical questions, and take initiative to pursue struggles and organize effectively. An important layer of individuals in these areas were worker intellectuals, thinkers whose development came not through formal education, but from the debates, discussion and educational activities tied to activism. This infrastructure provided the means to sustain memories, learn lessons and take action. (2005: 32–33)

As this suggests, a thriving infrastructure of dissent produces worker activists with abilities to organize and analyze. People like this energize and sustain a movement. In contrast, a weak infrastructure of dissent will lead to a movement that is weak at the grassroots, even if it is made up of formal organizations with an impressive number of members.

The working-class infrastructures of dissent that developed between the mid-1800s and mid-1900s melted away in the second half of the twentieth century. The right-wing climate and movement purges of the Cold War dealt a big blow to the radical left, both Communists and the left wing of the CCF. "Responsible" bureaucratic unionism with its "obey now, grieve later" stance stifled the informal organization of activists in workplaces. During the economic boom that followed the Second World War, many long-standing working-class neighbourhoods where wage-earners had lived close to their workplaces changed dramatically as people moved away to new suburbs from which they drove to work by car (Sears 2005). The New Left of the 1960s and 1970s in Canada sank few roots in the working class. In Quebec, some new infrastructures of dissent developed during the working-class radical-ization of the 1960s and 1970s (Mills 2010) but these did not endure. The restructuring of capitalism after the end of the post-war boom, discussed below, further weakened the remaining infrastructures. For example, "when plants close and workers 'relocate,' it is not only individual workers that are uprooted. The relationships and common workplace-neighourhood histo-ries out of which class consciousness emerges are fractured and dispersed" (Gindin 1998a: 80).

Today, infrastructures of dissent are very weak or absent altogether. There are very few caucuses or informal groups of activists within unions who come together to advance their kind of unionism. The radical left is very small and dispersed. It also lacks roots in the working class, being "very much centred in the university" with a "real disconnect from working people."[4] There are no longer institutions that promote workers' capacity for collective action on a significant scale. There are fewer places where people from different workplaces, unions or other organizations can get to know each other face-to-face, even though the Internet has created some new opportunities for communication and networking (for example, the site <autoworker.net>). The case of Winnipeg's Union Centres is revealing. Even in the 1970s, the Union Centre on Portage Avenue was a place where members of different unions and other activists gathered to drink, play shuffleboard and talk politics, with the numbers swelling during strikes and important rounds of collective bargaining.[5] The new Union Centre that opened on Broadway Avenue in 1990 houses the offices of many Manitoba and Winnipeg union bodies. It is simply a headquarters for the labour officialdom, not a home for a community of activists. Similarly, few neighbourhoods cultivate the capacity for collective action that was evident in the Great Depression when people mobilized to block the eviction of their neighbours. However, some of this does exist today in certain urban neighbourhoods where large numbers of recent immigrants live and share common experiences of racism and poverty (for example, Somali immigrants in Etobicoke have mobilized against racist policing).[6]

As a result of the dwindling of infrastructures of dissent, "longer-term relationships [between workers] that develo[p] collective capacities to act as a class" (Sears 2005: 33) rarely exist today. The kind of lively informal learning, discussion and networking that once took place in the working-class movement is now much less common. Lessons learned by previous genera-tions of activists are rarely passed down. All this affects the movement in many ways. Workers usually lack the means to collectively assess the attacks they face and to analyze defeats and victories in order to draw lessons for the future. Few of today's union members have experienced, for example, mobilizing coworkers to oppose the ratification of a tentative agreement, and so this is rarely seen as possible. There is little ability in the rank-and-file to take initiatives independently of official leaders when they are providing ineffective direction, as seen in many situations, including the Ontario Days of Action (Camfield 2000), the HEU strike of 2004 (Camfield 2006) and the Toronto municipal strike of 2009. Without a vibrant infrastructure of dissent, it has been very difficult for active members of the working-class movement to understand and resist the ruling-class offensive that has been part of the restructuring of capitalism.

Capitalist Restructuring

Between the late 1940s and the mid-1970s, global capitalism experienced a remarkable period of sustained economic growth. So significant was this boom that it misled many people into thinking capitalism's traditional pattern of booms and slumps had been overcome. But falling profit rates brought the long post-war boom to an end with a global recession in 1974–1975. Unemployment and inflation rose. Capitalists and governments searched for ways to restore corporate profits and power, both of which had declined. "No one really knew or understood with any certainty what kind of answer would work and how." Eventually, "through a series of gyrations and chaotic experiments" (Harvey 2005: 13), they came up with a way of trying to reorganize capitalism to achieve their aims: neoliberalism.[7] There are many aspects of neoliberalism, but at its core is dismantling or at least weakening anything that acts as a barrier to capitalist profit-making. These barriers include employment standards, social programs that assist the unemployed, union collective agreements, state-owned enterprises, controls on investment or trade and rules that prevent for-profit firms from operating in some sectors (for example, provincial bans on companies selling medical services that are provided to citizens under the non-profit medicare system in Canada and Quebec) or that regulate business activity (such as environmental protection regulations). Implementing the neoliberal restructuring agenda required a stepping-up of the offensive by employers and states against the working class that had begun in the mid-1970s.

In Canada and Quebec (as in countries around the world), this offensive has struck many blows to the working class. Pattern bargaining, in which one bargaining settlement is accepted as the standard for settlements at other employers in the same industry, has "broken down" (Tucker 2004: 110) in most industries where it existed as employers have sought to cut costs and pit workers in different locations within an industry against each other.[8] Jobs have been cut on a large scale, especially in the private sector. What were formerly the two biggest private sector unions were hit hard. Between 1967 and 1985, total United Auto Workers membership in the U.S. and Canada fell by 32.6 percent while the USW lost no less than 40.6 percent of its members (High 2003: 146). The recession of the early 1980s was more severe in the U.S. than north of the border, where many small- and medium-sized manufacturing facilities closed rather than large ones (167). However, "thousands of unionized jobs disappeared in the 1990s when a tidal wave of plant closings and mass lay-offs struck" Canada and Quebec (196). In manufacturing alone, 338,000 jobs were lost between 1989 and 1992 (195). Many of the factory jobs created later in the decade were soon wiped out. More than 772,000 manufacturing jobs were eliminated between August 2002 and early 2009, amounting to 30 percent of the manufacturing workforce. A full 337,000 of the losses took place in late 2008 and early 2009. Across sectors, employers cut more than 400,000 full-time jobs between October 2008 and April 2009 (Campbell 2009). The union presence declined in the private sector as some firms shut down or were bought up, others restructured and new jobs were created by non-unionized employers. Union density in the private sector dropped from 29.8 percent in 1981 (Morissette, Schellenberg and Johnson 2005) to 16.1 percent in 2008 (Statistics Canada 2009); private sector workers are now *much* less likely to have any kind of union protection than public sector workers.

In this context, employers have had great success in reorganizing workplaces in ways that "undermine the creation of connections and networks in the workplace" (Richardson 2008: 70), out of which solidarity is built, and in compelling workers to comply with demands to work harder (Rinehart 2006: 157–63). Sometimes, as we have seen, they have been assisted by union officials who have bought into the idea of partnership with employers. Non-unionized employers have taken advantage of this climate of insecurity and fear to hone "human resource management" schemes designed to help them deter and defeat efforts to unionize.[9]

The fear of losing one's job has been made worse by the difficulty of finding a new job that offers full-time hours, at least the same hourly pay and the relative stability of an open-ended contract with one employer. Average hourly real wages (wages adjusted for inflation) have been stagnant since the late 1970s (Russell and Dufour 2007). As a result, the main ways for people to increase their buying power have been working longer hours (for example, in a two-parent household, the mother of a small child working for wages full-time rather than part-time) and going deeper into debt — the average total debt per household was 140 percent of disposable income in 2008, up from 91 percent in 1990 (Sauvé 2009: 11). Temporary employment, fixed-term contracts, part-time jobs and situations in which people who, in reality, are wage-workers are legally classified as self-employed (and therefore denied the minimum legal rights of employees) have all increased. The proportion of wage-earners with full-time "permanent" jobs (whose contracts do not have a fixed end date) decreased from 67 percent to 63 percent between 1989 and 2003. For men, the decline was from 71 percent to 66 percent and for women from 63 percent to 59 percent (Vosko 2006: 22). Workers of colour, particularly women of colour, are over-represented in precarious jobs (Galabuzi 2006: 128–29). Whether in standard or precarious employment, the Monday-to-Friday daytime schedule for paid work is less and less common: more people are working variable shifts, in the evening or overnight and/or on weekends (Shalla 2007). The pressure to stay in or accept a bad job has been intensified by the deliberate weakening of unemployment insurance by federal governments. Renamed Employment Insurance (EI) in the mid-1990s, EI provides benefits that are more measly than in the past to only about four in ten unemployed wage-earners (CLC 2009). Provincial governments' attacks on social assistance (Workman 2009: 107–18) have also been designed to "make people desperate enough to take any job that comes along" (118).

Working people have also been loaded with greater demands that stem from how the neoliberal restructuring of capitalism has reshaped society outside the workplace and how this affects the world of working for wages. This is especially true for families where adults have children and/or other adults to care for. Caregiving responsibilities have increased as elderly people live longer and health care cuts result in people being sent home sooner and sicker. This growing burden of care falls disproportionately on the shoulders of women. Having to juggle different and often irregular schedules of paid work along with child care; getting children to and from school, sports and other scheduled activities; taking elderly parents to appointments and buying groceries — to name just some of the most common demands on the time of working-class people — has created a stressful time squeeze. Among other things, this harried way of living has "a way of suppressing feelings and ideas that might challenge the status quo or the market culture" and "inhibits the individual from thinking about non-busybee issues…, such as why one is so busy, and the purpose behind it, as well as the state of the larger society" (Hothschild 2007: 6).

These conditions of work and life — stressful, squeezed for time and insecure — have been brought about by the neoliberal restructuring of capitalism. The working-class movement's resistance to neoliberalism has been generally weak. The leaders of the traditional party of the Canadian left, the NDP, have come to accept neoliberalism (discussed below). So too has most of the union officialdom. It is no surprise, then, that the neoliberal message that *There Is No Alternative* (TINA), to use former British Prime Minister Margaret Thatcher's phrase, has come to seem "common sense" to many working-class people. This leaves them "open to blaming others," such as immigrants and unions, for their problems and to "supporting right-wing policies" (Luxton and Corman 2001: 256). As government-funded programs decline, unions weaken and people move in search of work, more people end up relying purely on individualistic or family-centred ways of getting by. As this happens, they devote less time and energy to broader friendship networks, community groups and unions. The weakening of these ties and organizations only reinforces people's inward-looking focus on their families (265). In short, capitalist restructuring has significantly weakened the working class as a social force, reducing unity, solidarity and the capacity to resist.

The impact of all this on the working-class movement has been very damaging. Bureaucratic "responsible" unions whose members had gained better wages and benefits during the post-war boom years of high profits and low unemployment through negotiations and strikes (including wildcats) were unprepared for the ruling-class offensive and restructuring. Militants who were used to fighting for more than employers wanted to give were disoriented by demands that workers give back past gains and by governments that ran roughshod over collective bargaining rights by passing laws that broke strikes and imposed settlements (Panitch and Swartz 2003). The Cold

War purge and the withering of the infrastructure of dissent had deprived the movement of political resources. Activists who recognized that economic crises are inevitable under capitalism, that the state is not neutral and that workers need to engage in mass direct action if they want to win could have helped other workers to understand what was happening and to resist the coming of neoliberalism. "Only strikes, sit-ins, sustained general strikes and marches backed by clearly articulated political messages could have stemmed the neoliberal tide" (Workman 2009: 132). Unfortunately, there were few people in the movement who understood this outside Quebec; in Quebec, those who did proved unable to act as an effective force to promote militant opposition.[10]

Neoliberalism has pummeled the working-class movement. As I argued earlier, concession bargaining has corroded the basic idea of unionism — in the words of an old maxim, "you don't need a union to go backward." The loss of unionized jobs has deprived some unions of many activists. As the balance of power in the workplace has tilted even more in employers' favour, the confidence that some workers (for example, many in CUPW) once had to engage in direct action on the job has evaporated. The onslaught also pushed many union officials into closer collaboration with employers. Many have accepted two-tier contracts and other concessions that further divide workers. Intensified competition between firms has encouraged private sector unionists to get on board with their bosses' schemes in the hope of saving jobs. Neoliberal restructuring of the public sector encourages public sector unionists to do much the same. As workers' expectations have fallen, so, too, has support for collective action — the heart of working-class movements. Years of retreat under the blows of neoliberalism have left many people with the belief that resistance is futile. This is what some have called the "TINA Syndrome." Approaches based on workers fighting back, such as mobilization unionism, social movement unionism and direct action by anti-poverty and other groups based outside the workplace, usually appear extremely unrealistic to most working-class people. None of this encourages people to be active in unions or other movement groups. This helps explain the falling levels of participation in many movement organizations. With an ageing population and inadequate health care, child care and home care programs, some women activists are increasingly having to "pull back from pretty much everything" because of the demands of "taking care of ageing parents and grandchildren and so forth."[11] The decline of the political forces that might have been expected to criticize neoliberalism and argue for alternatives has further reinforced the TINA attitude.

Sundown on the Left?

Left-wing parties and other political groups — those that seek the replacement of capitalism or at least reforms that improve the lives of the working class and oppressed people within capitalist society — have historically been a source of strength for working-class movements around the world (and vice versa: working-class movements and other social justice movements have nourished the political left). By promoting ideas of social and economic equality, democracy, collective action and criticism of corporate rule, they have encouraged people who have little wealth or power to believe the status quo is unjust and needs to be changed. People committed to left-wing political visions that give unions and other workers' organizations an important role have played key leadership roles in organizing their fellow workers and keeping movement organizations going through hard times.

For this reason, the decline since the 1970s of the main political currents of the global left has affected working-class movements, including the movement in Canada and Quebec. Reformist social democratic parties like the NDP and the Labour Party in Britain, which pledged to bring in social reforms when elected to government, have capitulated to neoliberalism and implemented it when in office. "Communist" parties that looked to the U.S.S.R. as a model for an alternative to capitalism have disappeared or dwindled into insignificance as the bureaucratic dictatorships that called themselves "Communist" have collapsed or shifted to "free market" capitalism under one-party rule. The "Third World" national development project has also succumbed to the neoliberal onslaught (Singer 1999; Prashad 2007). The small currents of anti-capitalist radicalism and the revolutionary far left that grew in the global radicalization from the mid-1960s to the mid-1970s have also declined. Since the mid-1990s, resistance to neoliberalism centred in Latin America and, to a lesser extent, Western Europe has revived the desire and will to seek radical change, but the fledgling new left is still weak (McNally 2006). In Canada and Quebec, the decline of the left has been one factor in the crumbling of the infrastructure of dissent discussed above. This section looks at other aspects of how the decline of the left has affected the working-class movement.

Since its creation in 1961, the NDP has been the only mass force on the left in Canada; it has always been a very minor player in Quebec. By the time the NDP was formed, the CPC had been reduced to a small rump by Cold War anti-communism and the revulsion of many of its members at the U.S.S.R.'s crushing of the 1956 revolution in Hungary (Penner 1988). In Quebec, the PQ has always had a social democratic wing, but was never a party of the left. The Green Party formed in the 1980s was not on the left except in a couple of provinces, and its politics have become solidly neoliberal (Sharzer 2007).

In the late twentieth century "across Canada the NDP's postwar vision of social democracy has been called into question and has undergone a significant transition" (Cooke 2007: 1). The NDP was once a party that advocated social reforms, kept some distance from corporations and was proud to be the political arm of the union officialdom (social democratic politics and "responsible" unionism share a common logic of trying to harmonize the interests of labour and capital within the existing social order and legal framework). It has become a party whose leaders accept the straightjacket of neoliberalism as the framework for policy, do their best to cozy up to business and try to keep some distance from unions.[12] "The ideological principle of *rejecting* the Liberals ha[s] faded in the face of the electoral principle of wanting to *replace* the Liberals" (Gindin 1998b: 14). The continued existence of the NDP as a separate party has at least kept more union officials and rank-and-file activists from falling into the kind of dependence on the Liberals that exists between U.S. unions and the Democrats. Devotion to the openly corporate Democratic Party has been extremely harmful for unions and other social movements in the U.S. (Moody 2007: 143–68; Davis 1986: 52–101). But the federal NDP's campaign in 2008 is revealing about what the party has become. It

> remained silent on the key pillars of neoliberalism — corporate power, privatization, financial deregulation, free trade, precarious work and the radical transfer of income from labour to capital.... We were even treated to the absurd spectacle of the NDP leader [Jack Layton] — in the midst of a historic meltdown of financial markets and credible predictions of the worst economic downturn in generations — refusing to even countenance the very idea of running a government deficit, just as neoliberal governments here and abroad prepared to do just that. (Rao 2008)

Many provincial leaders of the NDP are even more conservative than their federal counterparts. Although a considerable number of NDP activists have been unhappy about how the NDP has evolved, there has been no left-wing challenge within the party significant enough to cause its establishment any worry since the defeat of the short-lived New Politics Initiative at the 2001 federal NDP convention (Rao 2004).

The party's adaptation to neoliberal capitalism is not just a matter of what is written in party platforms or said in media appearances. NDP governments in B.C., Saskatchewan, Manitoba, Ontario, the Yukon and Nova Scotia in the 1990s and the first decade of this century have in no way challenged neoliberalism. The Ontario NDP government (1990–1995) led by Bob Rae not only quickly abandoned many promised reforms, but imposed a "Social Contract" of pay freezes, unpaid days off and layoffs on public sector workers. Its misdeeds also included a crackdown on alleged "welfare fraud" and the prosecution of three CUPW members for strike activity (Panitch and Swartz 2003: 166–77). The Saskatchewan NDP, in office from 1991 to 2007, "continued and in fact expanded the policies of neoliberalism" initiated by their Tory predecessors in the 1980s (Warnock 2005: 83). Similarly, the Manitoba NDP, in office since 1999, has maintained continuity with the previous Conservative government by retaining its balanced budget legislation and by cutting taxes (Gonick 2007). In Nova Scotia, the party leadership's strategy as it sailed to victory in the 2009 provincial election was to "curb expectations of progressives in the province" (Saulnier 2009); in office, the NDP has done nothing to rock the neoliberal boat.

NDP influence on the working-class movement has always promoted relying exclusively on the parliamentary road to social change. When in opposition, NDP leaders are fearful that anything more than mild-mannered protests against right-wing governments will cost them votes and respectability. This was clear in the hostility of NDP leaders to the Days of Action in Ontario and the extra-parliamentary fight-backs in B.C. against the Social Credit government in the early 1980s and the Liberals two decades later (Palmer 1987; Herring 2002; Camfield 2006). The NDP's rightward shift has reinforced the hold of the TINA Syndrome within the working-class movement. As the NDP plays the dumbed-down, corporate media-driven game of official politics and accepts its strict definition of what policies are acceptable, it helps narrow rather than expand people's ideas about society and politics. NDP leaders are part of the neoliberal consensus that stretches all the way to the most reactionary fringe of the Conservatives. This means their influence on unions and other movement groups is a pull to the right. Their acceptance of neoliberalism lowers people's expectations and amplifies the TINA message.

Even worse, NDP governments have "actively undermined union power and solidarity" (Panitch and Swartz 2003: 178). The party apparatus consciously tries to get union officials and social justice groups to support whatever an NDP government does. The party's current and historic ties to unions give it a lot of sway within them, especially with labour's top brass. To the extent that the NDP in office is able to get the working-class movement to do what the government desires, the NDP undermines the movement's independence and weakens resistance to neoliberalism. In Ontario, the Social Contract deeply divided the workers' movement because leaders of the provinces' private sector unions, except the CAW, backed this attack on public sector workers out of loyalty to the NDP. The election of the NDP in Manitoba in 1999 was followed by the complete demobilization of the province's unions, leading to a stultifying complacency and inaction. In Saskatchewan, the NDP used back-to work legislation against striking workers at Saskatchewan Power

Corporation in late 1998 and nurses (who defied the law and won anyway) in 1999 (201–202). The B.C. NDP government did the same against teachers in 1993 and other school board workers in 2000 (204, 206).

As for the radical left, its small size even in the 1970s, except in Quebec, meant that its decline — along with the rest of the infrastructure of dissent to which it was connected — had only a minor impact on the working-class movement. In Quebec, the effect was more dramatic: the rapid collapse of the sizeable radical left in the early 1980s was followed by a sharp right turn in the movement.

Until the collapse of Stalinism in the U.S.S.R. and Eastern Europe at the close of the 1980s, the CPC still had some influence among union and social justice activists, particularly in B.C. It challenged business unionism, but not bureaucracy. It had long been subservient in practice to labour's official leaders, as was made clear by its role in the debacle of the Operation Solidarity movement of extra-parliamentary protest in B.C. in 1983 (Palmer 1987). The hard work of socialist feminists and other feminists in unions in Canada and Quebec did reduce the level of sexism in the movement and push it in a more anti-sexist direction. The decline of the women's movement in the 1990s (Rebick 2005) has reduced their numbers and some of their gains have been lost. The Canadian Centre for Policy Alternatives, other left-leaning think-tanks and the Council of Canadians have given active union members analysis to challenge the claims of neoliberal ideology. This has probably helped bolster the resolve of hard-pressed activists to keep up the fight in hard times. Anti-capitalist radicals have too little presence in unions to have any impact outside of a handful of locals, though they have more influence in the various other small activist groups of the movement.

The NDP's impact on the working-class movement, then, is to reinforce "responsible" bureaucratic unionism and the acceptance of neoliberal capitalism while encouraging verbal opposition to regressive government policies when the NDP is not in office. The NDP does not educate and inspire people to become activists in the movement. It also discourages extra-parliamentary political action by workers. The fact that it exists acts as a barrier to more of the movement aligning with the Liberals (the leading party of Canadian capitalism in the twentieth century and currently Bay Street's second choice), but the party's adaptation to neoliberalism fuels rather than challenges the TINA Syndrome among workers. The left outside the NDP once contributed to pockets of radicalism within the movement; today its impact is minimal.

The Direction Taken

The final force responsible for giving the movement its current shape is the direction given it by the full-time officers and staff at the head of the unions. The peak of the labour officialdom deserves some specific attention; its role should not be obscured by the other forces discussed in this chapter. It is true that most high-level full-time officers and staff do not have much ability to change their unions in dramatic ways, even if they wanted to do so (which few do). The forces discussed so far in this chapter deeply shape unions and have a big influence on how top officers and staff act. Top officials in the more centralized unions, such as the CAW, have only limited power to alter the organizations they head by themselves, as the occasional would-be reformer elected to a top position soon discovers.[13] Their counterparts in more decentralized unions, of which CUPE is the best example, have less. Central labour bodies from the level of the CLC and Quebec's labour federations down to local labour councils have little ability to weld affiliated unions together in joint action (Yates 2007: 69–70). Nevertheless, top leaders and key staff do make choices about how to respond to developments and what path to chart that have some effect on what kind of organizations unions are.

Today the officialdom is, on the whole, more ossified and probably more bureaucratic than it has ever been.[14] The unions are headed by "a more and more entrenched layer of labour officialdom that owe[s] both its material well-being and privileges as well as its broad political allegiance to the legalistic [framework]... of the post-World War II industrial order" (Palmer 2003: 487). This official leadership has been doggedly loyal to the bureaucratic labour relations framework laid down in the 1940s, even though governments have been violating it for decades (Panitch and Swartz 2003). It is preoccupied with preserving union institutions and its control within them. Carol Wall's saying in her 2005 outsider bid for the presidency of the CLC, that many top leaders "came to do good, but stayed to do well" (in Levant 2005: 5), rings true. Along with this goes an acceptance of giving up past gains to employers without a serious fight. CLC president Ken Georgetti sees lobbying government "as the way to get things done."[15] The actions of most national presidents and other high-ranking union leaders are consistent with this uncritical faith in parliamentary politics, which persists even though this approach has achieved so little for workers over the last forty years. Few have shown themselves willing to even occasionally try to mobilize workers' power against aggressive employers and governments or to openly criticize the NDP's shift to the right. As we have seen, the CAW's top leaders abandoned their mobilization unionist orientation. There are no equivalents in Canada or Quebec to, for example, militant British union presidents Bob Crow and Mark Serwotka, outspoken socialists who led strikes against the Labour Party government and supported left challenges to Labour in the first decade of the twenty-first century, despite the persistent loyalty of the leadership of the Trades Union Congress (British equivalent of the CLC) to the now deeply-neoliberal Labour Party.[16] Nor has any wing of the officialdom tried to change the movement from above in limited ways, as happened in the

U.S. in the second half of the 1990s (Moody 2007: 129–42; Fletcher and Gapasin 2008: 69–120). John Cartwright, head of the TYRLC, stands out as unusual because he is a prominent full-time official with a mobilization unionist approach, which he has put into practice at Toronto's labour council (discussed in Chapter Eight) and with his unsuccessful "Action Agenda" for the 2008 CLC convention (Wilmot 2008a).[17]

When the level of resistance to neoliberalism has risen — as in the Ontario Days of Action and the protests and strikes in B.C. in 2002–2005 and Quebec in 2003 — no section of the union officialdom has tried to escalate it to the level needed to win victories (Camfield 2000, 2005, 2006, 2009a). In most of the rare cases when groups of workers have really fought to win and had victories in their grasp that would have given hope and inspiration to many, officials have actively reigned in workers because they feared losing control of "their" members and the possible penalties from the courts. Two glaring examples are the 1995 wildcat by 120 Calgary hospital laundry workers that sparked walkouts by over 2500 other health care workers (Reshef and Rastin 2003: 156–59) and the HEU strike in B.C. in 2004 (Camfield 2006).[18] As one Alberta union officer involved in the Calgary wildcat admitted, "[the members] were demobilized. And I know, because I was part of the process of demobilization" (in Reshef and Rastin 2003: 158). The simple perpetuation of union institutions is the goal to which most top union officers and staff have devoted themselves, at great cost to unions as organizations through which workers can act in their own interests.

This is no surprise when we recall what was argued earlier about why full-time officials tend to treat preserving union institutions as an end in itself, quite apart from what the union means for its worker members. One additional reason why some peak officials in Canada and Quebec have been so conservative is that small numbers of them have become capitalists. The people in question have come to be simultaneously labour officials and capitalists through their involvement on the boards of directors of Labour Sponsored Investment Funds (LSIFs) or with corporations set up using union pension funds. The most prominent of the latter is B.C.'s Concert Properties, a development firm owned by union and management pension plans whose assets were worth over $1.3 billion in 2009. Concert was originally set up in 1989 as VLC Properties, with Ken Georgetti (then president of the B.C. Federation of Labour) centrally involved (Offley 2004). Most of the members of its board are current or former full-time union officials.[19] Georgetti only resigned from Concert's board in 2004 after it was revealed the company had donated more than $16,000 to the B.C. Liberals.[20]

LSIFs are a kind of venture capital fund subsidized from tax revenue and sponsored by a union. They make what are "generally high risk, speculative investments" (Globe Investor 2009) in small- and medium-sized firms, typically in newer high-technology industries, and have been "the primary mechanism supporting entrepreneurial finance in Canada" (Cumming 2009).[21] LSIFs first developed in Quebec, with the Solidarity Fund created in 1983 by the CLC's Quebec wing, the Quebec Federation of Labour (QFL). The timing was significant: the crushing defeat inflicted by the PQ government on the Common Front of public sector unions in early 1983 signaled that the era of militancy and radicalism in Quebec labour was over (Palmer 1992: 362–65).[22] This opened the door for a very different kind of initiative by the leaders of a federation that a decade earlier had endorsed radical policies. Today, the Solidarity Fund remains the leading LSIF, with assets of $6.4 billion in 2009.[23] Most members of its board of directors are top QFL officers. The president of Quebec's third-largest union federation, the Centrale des syndicats du Québec, is also on the Solidarity Fund's board, while the Confédération des syndicats nationaux (CSN) has its own fund, Fondaction. The largest LSIF outside Quebec is GrowthWorks. GrowthWorks is part of the B.C.-headquartered Working Enterprises group of companies "owned by a coalition of B.C. labour unions" (Spika 2004).[24] GrowthWorks had assets of approximately one billion dollars in 2009.[25] Other LSIFs have not fared so well. For example, Crocus, sponsored by the Manitoba Federation of Labour, collapsed and was taken into receivership in 2005 (CBCnews.ca 2009b).

LSIFs "have diverted the energies and creativity of the sponsoring labour organizations." The main goal of LSIFs is the expansion of their capital. This "plants the seeds for a conflict of interest" whose "long-run political implications... are worrisome" (Stanford 1999: 35, 37). It is in the interests of union officials in their role as capitalist directors of LSIFs to support neoliberal measures that create a social environment in which corporate rates of profit rise, even though such measures hurt the working class. As these officials become more involved in business networks, they increasingly make decisions purely for the sake of LSIF profits and associate with people who, from the point of view of many union activists, are strange bedfellows. A case in point is the Solidarity Fund's support for Quebecor CEO Pierre Karl Péladeau's failed bid to buy the Montreal Canadians in 2009. This took place while CSN members at the *Journal de Montréal* were locked-out by Péladeau — the fourteenth lockout at one of his firms in fourteen years, as a CUPW activist pointed out in an open letter to QFL members. The letter accused Michel Arsenault, head of the QFL and chair of the Fund's board, of choosing to back the Fund's returns instead of the locked-out workers (Frappier 2009b). Such behaviour is predictable. By placing high-ranking union officials in positions where they objectively function as capitalists, involvement with the boards of LSIFs and companies like Concert Properties has had the effect of linking small numbers of union officials even more closely to business.

This has made parts of the officialdom in Canada and Quebec even more conservative.

Together, these forces — the transformation of unionism in the 1940s, the crumbling of the infrastructure of dissent, neoliberal capitalist restructuring, the decline of the left and the direction taken by the top union officials who have the most power within the movement — go a long way towards explaining why the working-class movement has come to be in the shape it is in. Part Two of this book is devoted to considering why and how the movement needs to change and examining how the kind of change needed might be achieved, building on the analysis of the movement developed in Part One.

Notes

1. On developments in the 1940s, see Palmer 1992, Heron 1996, Fudge and Tucker 2001, McInnis 2002 and Camfield 2002, on which this section draws.
2. Interview with John Friesen, November 19, 2008.
3. On the insurgent challenges within unions in the 1960s and early 1970s, see Palmer 2009 and Mills 2010.
4. Interview with John Friesen, November 19, 2008.
5. E-mail from Dave Hall to author, September 10, 2009. Hall was a union member active on the left in Winnipeg in the 1970s.
6. I owe this example to a conversation with OCAP organizer John Clarke in May 2009.
7. A great deal has been written about neoliberalism. For good introductions, see Harvey 2005, McNally 2010 and Saad-Filho and Johnston 2005.
8. For the case of meatpacking, see Forrest 1989.
9. Magna is a good example (Lewchuk and Wells 2006).
10. There were a few thousand activists on the far left in Quebec in the late 1970s, but most were divided into rival political groups that often behaved in ways that repulsed rather than attracted other people and that were organized in authoritarian and undemocratic ways. Many radicals in Quebec (as elsewhere) looked to China and Albania for inspiration and saw Stalin and Mao as great revolutionary thinkers. Dogmatic theory, undemocratic sect organization and illusions about states that, in reality, were anti-working class bureaucratic dictatorships and about short-term prospects for revolutionary change in North America contributed to the rapid collapse of the far left in Quebec in the early 1980s. See Moreau 1986 and Warren 2007.
11. Interview with Atlantic labour staffer, July 10, 2009.
12. The articles on the NDP in several provinces in Carroll and Ratner 2005 describe this shift to the right.
13. The case of Sudbury miner Dave Patterson's experience as director of District 6 of the USW is a prime example (Palmer 1992: 401; McKeigan 2008: 249–50).
14. Here I draw on Camfield 2009b.
15. Anonymous interview, June 11, 2009.
16. See, for example, Thomson and Sylvester 2009 and Mulholland 2004. I do not mean to suggest that these leaders are beyond criticism, but they clearly have no Canadian or Quebeçois counterparts.
17. See <labouraction.ca>.
18. The B.C. teachers' strike of 2005 was a partial exception: CUPE-B.C. leaders did

organize limited sympathy strikes but most of the rest of the union officialdom did nothing to mobilize the kind of action that could have helped the teachers win (Camfield 2009a). For a case of a determined strike that CUPE brass did not try to reign in, see Kuhling 2002.

19. As of September 2009, a majority of the board of directors of Concert Properties were union officials or held positions with union pension plans <www.concertproperties. com>.

20. Letter to Officers, B.C. Federation of Labour from James R Brown, Jack McCamy, Gene McGuckin, Will Offley, Jeff Pazik, Susan Roth and Sharyn Sigurdur, November 20, 2005.

21. The Ontario government has removed its subsidies for LSIFs, introduced under the NDP in 1992 (Cumming 2009).

22. According to Quebec CUPW activist Andre Frappier, the Solidarity Fund approach was advanced by top union officials at this time as an alternative to the left's call for shorter hours of work with no loss of pay, which had gained some support within QFL unions as a response to high unemployment.

23. As reported on its website <www.fondsftq.com> in September 2009.

24. According to the website of Working Enterprises Tax Services Ltd. <www.wetax. ca/about-us> the union bodies that own the holding company Working Enterprises Ltd. are the B.C. Federation of Labour, USW, CUPE-B.C., B.C. Government and Service Employees' Union, Canadian Office and Professional Employees Local 378, Health Sciences Association of B.C., UFCW Local 1518, International Longshore and Warehouse Union — Canada and the TWU.

25. As reported on its website <www.growthworks.ca> in September 2009.

Part Two

Looking Forward

7. Why Reinvent the Movement?

Faced with the reality of the working-class movement as it exists today, many people ask why they should care about it. Even veteran union activists can be tempted to throw in the towel. Without a doubt, unions in Canada and Quebec are, for the most part, pale[1] and stale. The official leadership is also usually male. Although men no longer outnumber women among union members, they still do in the labour officialdom. Unions whose officials cave in to employers' demands for concessions, treat members like children and do little or nothing to address many problems in workers' lives do not inspire people to devote their time and energy to labour's cause.

With this in mind, this chapter begins by asking the question "what good are working-class movements?" Answering this question involves a different kind of analysis than the rest of this book: a short reflection on what is good for human beings and an examination of how workers' movements are relevant to this good. This should give skeptical readers reasons for caring about the movement. The chapter, then, argues why and in what ways the movement in Canada and Quebec should change. What is called for is not just a more energetic or modified version of the movement as it exists today. Change needs to go deeper. The movement needs to be reinvented, just as it was reinvented in the opening decades of the twentieth century.

What Good are Working-Class Movements?

> Improvements in human life require social struggle. (Coburn 2009: 41)

What is Good?

Philosophers have long debated the question of what is good. John McMurtry observes that today we experience a paradox. On the one hand, the dominant ideal of the good life is that everyone has their own conception of what is good. On the other, in reality, the value of *"anything and everything is, no less and no more, the price it can get in global market exchange"* (McMurtry n.d.: 1.10). In response, McMurtry proposes connecting ethics (inquiry into what is good) with what human beings require to live (our life-requirements) and to flourish (the development of our capabilities). This life-ground approach to ethics is a powerful way of thinking about what is good. Unlike most philosophy today, it takes the real needs of flesh and blood humanity and the Earth's ecosystems seriously and does not shy away from being extremely critical of how contemporary society is organized.

As Jeff Noonan puts it, "living things, and human beings most of all, strive to maintain those connections with their life-requirements that enable them to live, to be healthy, and to more fully realize and enjoy their vital capabilities in society with others" (Noonan 2008a: 4). McMurtry explains,

> *Life* means organic movement, sentience and feeling, and thought. *Means of life* refers to whatever enables life to be preserved or to extend its vital range on these three planes of being alive. Clean air, food, water, shelter, affective interaction, environmental space, and accessible learning conditions are all means of life. To reproduce life-values is to hold these capacities at their established scope. To increase life-value is to widen or deepen them to a more comprehensive range... The more of life's breadths and depths are accessible to us, the better our condition. The more they are diminished — for example, by unemployment, a polluted environment, or unaffordable higher education — the worse our condition becomes. (1998: 298)

From this perspective, then, what is good for people is what maintains or enhances life — our capabilities to move, think and feel. The good is universal; it is the same for everyone.

Yet *how* people develop their capabilities is "always an open question and will necessarily vary in differing contexts and among different people" (Noonan 2008b: 32). For example, playing sports, dancing and walking quickly are all ways of developing our human capability to move. The opposite of the good is what diminishes people's capabilities. Along with what is good being universal, we can see that oppression and exploitation are always bad. Oppression and exploitation always reduce people's capabilities in some way. For this reason, they always diminish life-value (32).

What are the life-requirements (needs) that people require in order to be able to move, think and feel? McMurtry distinguishes genuine needs from what people want, but do not truly need, with the formula "N is a need, if and only if, and to the extent that, deprivation of N always results in a reduction of organic capability" (McMurtry 1998: 164). Put simply, something is a need only to the extent that people's capability to move, feel or think is reduced when they do not have access to it. For example, if I am deprived of water, I will soon die; water is a need. If I am cut off from any caring relations with other human beings, my mental health will eventually suffer, even if I tell myself it does not matter that no one cares about me; care is a need. If I am not allowed to eat pie, I will be unhappy. However, I can reflect on my unhappiness and realize that I do not really need pie;

pie is not a life-requirement, although nutritious food is. As these examples suggest, there are different categories of needs.

The most basic kind of needs are physical life-requirements. Without these, people will either die or suffer from poor health. Physical needs include clean air, open space, light, clean water, nutritious food, physical activity, waste disposal, shelter and safety. Socio-cultural needs are another category of need. These are what people require in order not simply to survive but to function as members of an animal species that is distinguished from other animals by having consciousness. These life-requirements include education of some kind, care, play, meaningful work and political institutions that allow people to take part in decision-making about matters that affect their lives (Noonan 2008a: 6–7). The final category of life-requirements is the need for free time: "an experience of time itself as free, as an open matrix of human possibilities" (7). People need time in which they can freely develop their capabilities to feel, think and move. In order to have this experience, people need time away from paid work. However, simply having time away from paid work is not enough because in society today our time outside of work is not necessarily truly free time (Noonan 2009).[2]

How are these life-requirements relevant to what is good? They are directly relevant because they are means of life. People are able to preserve or expand their capabilities of feeling, moving and thinking only if they are able to meet their needs or in the process of meeting their needs (Noonan 2008a: 4). For instance, children need education to develop their thinking abilities. How children access the education they require can vary; attending public schools and home schooling are two different ways of meeting this need. But to develop their thinking capabilities, children must have access to education of some kind. Genuinely improving children's education increases their ability to think. This increases life-value and is therefore good.

Some life-requirements are needed by people in all times and places. For example, everyone needs clean water and nutritious food. These are universal physical needs, although people can satisfy the need for food in many different ways. Other life-requirements are needed by people because of how their particular society is organized, but would not be needed (or would be less necessary) if society were different. These are what Noonan calls instrumental system needs (Noonan 2008a: 6). For example, in Canada and Quebec today, the places where people work for pay are often far from where they live and are difficult or impossible to get to by public transit. As a result, many people need to have access to a car or other vehicle to get to work. However, this need would become much less important if bus, subway and train service were improved.

Working-Class Movements and What Is Good

The life-ground ethical perspective allows us to evaluate if workers' movements contribute to what is good. Do working-class movements enhance or at least preserve life value? Do they have an impact on the ability of people to satisfy their needs? What does social research tell us?

Perhaps the most obvious thing we know about unions is that they tend to raise workers' wages and win benefits from employers. The size of the union wage premium varies. In sectors or countries where collective agreement coverage is high, such as France, Denmark, Sweden, Norway and the public sector in Canada and Quebec today, the premium is lower. Where the percentage of workers covered by union contracts is low, as in the U.S. today, the premium is high. However, the size of the premium is hard to calculate. There is also another effect that the premium may miss: unions can indirectly raise the wages of non-union workers. In some cases employers of non-unionized workers offer higher wages than they otherwise would in order to match the pay of unionized workers, in the hope this will keep workers from unionizing. Unions also tend to resist moves by employers to cut wages, at least to some extent. In many countries, unions have also won benefits from employers ranging from health care for employees to pensions for retirees and their spouses.

In contemporary capitalist societies, most goods and services are commodities. In other words, they must be purchased and are available only to those who can afford to buy them. For this reason, most people need to work for wages in order to meet many of their physical needs. In some situations, such as where adults must pay for their children's education, wage income is also needed to guarantee that certain socio-cultural needs are met. Sometimes higher hourly wages also make it possible for people to work less, which creates the possibility of more free time. To be sure, making more money is not good in itself. Money itself does not preserve or enhance life. There is evidence that the consumerist drive to get more money in order to buy more stuff is bad for human health (Kasser 2003). But in a capitalist society, people need enough money to obtain whatever commodities they must buy in order to meet their life-requirements.

Beyond what we need in order to not be harmed, as McMurtry puts it in the passage quoted earlier, "the more of life's breadths and depths are accessible to us, the better our condition." When we realize our human capabilities, life-value is increased. This is good (provided that others are not harmed in the process). Unfortunately, in a capitalist society, people often need money in order to develop certain capabilities. For example, people are usually charged user fees (tuition) to get access to advanced education. Instruments, tools and other supplies needed to play music or make art generally cost money. It often costs money to play a sport at a high level of skill.

By raising wages and gaining other benefits, unions allow wage-earners covered by collective agreements and members of their households to have access to a higher level of goods and services with which to satisfy some of their life-requirements and develop some of their capabilities. Even in rich countries like Canada, people who do not have better-paid jobs often lack access to some life-requirements. Getting a unionized job can mean, for example, that a previously low-paid wage-earner in an expensive city is able to move from unhealthy to adequate housing and can afford to buy nutritious rather than poor-quality food for herself and her child. Benefit coverage along with higher wages gives people better access to health services that are generally not provided by the public health care system in Canada and Quebec, such as prescription drugs, physiotherapy, counselling and dentistry. People can use higher wages to access higher education and pursue interests that develop their human capabilities to move and think. Thus, we can conclude that working-class movements contribute to what is good to the extent that the better wages and benefits they win help people in capitalist societies to meet needs and to increase life-value by realizing their capabilities.

Related to this, working-class movements can also make a difference by helping wage-earners hang on to their jobs. They can sometimes win job security protection in collective agreements or in law that make it more difficult for employers to treat workers as disposable. No-layoff clauses in contracts are one example. Rules that limit the arbitrary power of bosses to fire workers are another (such rules are weak in Canada and the U.S., even for unionized workers, but many workers in Europe enjoy much greater protection thanks to stronger working-class movements). Severance pay and requirements to give notice before dismissing workers do not save jobs, but they soften the blow of job loss, at least a bit. This kind of job protection helps workers to meet their life-requirements by making it more difficult for them to be thrown out of paid work, or by compensating or delaying job loss.

Another way workers' movements matter in ethical terms is revealed by the evidence that points to a positive link between working-class power and better health outcomes for the population as a whole (Muntaner et al. 2004). As one health researcher has put it, "Class mobilisation and politics are critical for health and health inequalities, because progressive social and class movements and parties are the dynamic forces pushing for improvements in the human condition, rather than simply more of everything for the rich (Coburn 2009: 41). In the words of two other researchers, "In countries with weaker labor movements and social democratic parties and stronger capitalist classes... there has been a weaker commitment to redistributive policies and worse health indicators" (Navarro and Shi 2002: 417). Workers' movements tend to pressure governments to dedicate more resources to social programs (and to resist cuts to social spending). When this pressure influences what governments do, it has a positive impact on health: "Cross nationally, higher levels of social expenditures… are associated with greater life expectancy, lower maternal mortality, and a smaller proportion of low birthweight babies" (Lynch et al. 2000: 1203). In general, "the implementation of policies aimed at reducing social inequalities seems to have a salutary effect on population health" (Navarro et al. 2006: 1037). Implementing policies designed to boost corporate profits has the opposite effect: "Countries pursuing neo-liberal policies display far greater social inequalities" (Coburn 2004: 54), including health inequalities.

There are many examples of how workers' movements have demanded and won public services that improve people's health. For example, the often-militant struggle of unemployed workers who refused to "starve in silence" in Canada during the Great Depression of the 1930s was one of the pressures that led to the creation of federal Unemployment Insurance (UI) in 1940 (Struthers 1983). UI helped keep unemployed wage-earners and members of their families from becoming hungry and homeless, both of which are bad for health. In the 1950s and 1960s, unions and labour-backed committees supporting public health care did a significant part of the campaigning that eventually led to the 1966 federal Medical Care Act. The result was a pub-licly funded and delivered health care system (Buott 2009). In the countries of Northern Europe, where social programs have been and still are more extensive than in Canada and Quebec, "a strong and well-organized work-ers' movement has been and is a prerequisite for the Scandinavian welfare models" (Johannsson and Partanen 2004: 312). In these and many other cases, working-class movements have influenced the development of more and better social programs. Around the world, they have also resisted gov-ernment efforts to eliminate or weaken public health care, welfare, housing and unemployment insurance programs. Such programs give people access to services that enhance life-value. So we can say that workers' movements contribute to what is good to the extent that they have a positive influence on people's health.

Another way that workers' movements have a positive impact on health is by pushing employers to make workplaces safer and healthier and demand-ing that governments regulate workplaces to protect workers' health and safety (Smith 2000). This obviously makes a difference for wage-earners. For example, Danish painters' union activists played a leading role in identifying the harm caused by organic solvents and protecting workers from exposure to them (Johansson and Partanen 2004: 310). Controls on toxic substances in workplaces, such as asbestos and PCBs, can protect not only wage-earners who are at risk of being exposed to them but also other people and other species of life. Workers' power makes it more likely that health and safety rules will actually be enforced. The reverse is also true. The weakening of a working-class movement "may rapidly change workers' health situation for the worse, even when laws and regulations remain unchanged" (319). Improving health and safety is, then, another way in which workers' movements contribute to what is good.

In addition, when working-class movements are strong — stronger than in Canada and Quebec today — they tend to reduce the power of employers over wage-earners on the job, even if only to a small degree. Health research has shown that a low level of control by workers in the workplace, a high level of demands and a low level of support make work stressful for workers. This is bad for workers' health. So when management control of workers is reduced, wage-earners experience less unhealthy stress (Crinson and Yuill 2008: 465–66). Weakening management domination is a further way that working-class movement organizations can have a positive effect on human health.

It is good for workers' health to spend less time in demanding workplaces in which they have little control and support. Since capitalism first developed in England, unions and workers' parties in many parts of the world have fought successfully to shorten the working day and win more time away from the workplace in the form of vacations and general holidays. These gains "were not part of a natural progression of capitalist development," as is sometimes suggested. They were "the outcome of decades of struggle by workers to improve their conditions of employment and secure a greater amount of time outside of paid work" (Shalla 2007: 230). Shorter hours are not just good for workers' physical and mental health. Time away from paid work is important in its own right, since it creates the possibility that people who work for wages will be able to enjoy free time — another life-requirement of human beings.

Working-class movements are also capable of using their power to make other kinds of positive changes in society:

- Shelter and services. From before and during the Great Depression of the 1930s to the Great Recession that hit in 2008, movement groups in poor workers' communities have mobilized to block the eviction of people from their homes and defend poor people's access to water and electricity.[3] This kind of organizing is rare in Canada today, but it is a strong tradition in many countries, including South Africa, where organizations like the Western Cape Anti-Eviction Campaign are engaged in such struggles (see antieviction.org.za). By preserving people's access to shelter, water and other physical requirements of life, this contributes to the good.
- Equality. Unions have made collective bargaining gains that weaken oppression. For example, equal pay, pay equity (equal pay for work of

equal value) and anti-harassment provisions in collective agreements reduce the weight of gender inequality women suffer in sexist societies. Anti-discrimination provisions have also chipped away at racism and heterosexism. Extending spousal benefits to same-gender partners has promoted equality for LGBT people (Hunt and Rayside 2007). Since oppression always diminishes life-value, such gains are good.

- Democracy. After studying how liberal democracy came to replace completely undemocratic forms of government in countries around the world, three researchers have concluded that "the organized working class appeared as a key actor in the development of full democracy almost everywhere" (Rueschemeyer, Stephens and Stephens 1992: 270). Although liberal democracy is a very weak kind of democracy, if we take seriously the idea that democracy means rule by the people,[4] it is still a good in ethical terms. This is because there is very little scope for people to exercise their capabilities to act on issues of public concern if political institutions are not even weakly democratic.

- Social and ecological justice. Working-class organizations have, at times, taken action against ecological devastation or in support of struggles by other groups for social justice. In Australia in the 1970s, the New South Wales branch of the Builders' Labourers' Federation took direct action ("green bans") to block destructive development projects (Burgmann 1998). These workers "took it upon themselves to dispute employers' rights to build whatever they liked where they liked" (4). The 1990 Redwood Summer campaign by radical ecologist labour activists in California helped protect 2000-year-old redwood trees in Headwaters Forest (Shantz 2002). The "first significant breakthrough" for the international movement against apartheid in South Africa was the 1963 refusal of Danish dockworkers to unload South African goods (Vally 2008: 28), an action later copied by workers in other countries. In 2003, Italian rail unionists refused to work on trains carrying U.S. military equipment headed for use in the war on Iraq and helped anti-war protestors to delay these trains (Oliveri 2003). Such action preserves life-values threatened by ecological destruction and war or contributes to struggles against oppression. It is therefore good.

Finally, and more controversially, some argue that working-class movements have the potential to play a key role in fundamentally transforming capitalist society in ways that would eliminate the root causes of many threats to human needs and ensure people have access to the physical, socio-cultural and temporal requirements of life.[5] If they are correct, this would make workers' movements even more significant as a force for good.

Two Objections

Having presented this case for why working-class movements contribute to achieving and defending what is good, I will consider two challenges to it. The most common response to this line of argument would probably be to claim that working-class movements lower corporate profits. Whether or not this is true, this accusation carries no weight for anyone who accepts life-ground ethics. Quite simply, reducing profits does not diminish life-value, so it is not an ethical problem.

The challenge that cannot be dismissed so easily is the claim that working-class movements damage "the economy." By raising the cost of labour, they allegedly raise the level of unemployment. By threatening profits and even management's control in the workplace, they discourage capitalists from investing. When capitalists stop investing their capital in the production of goods and services, fewer goods and services will be produced and people may not be able to meet their needs. In short, workers' movements poison the goose that lays golden eggs and, as a result, cause harm to people.

This challenge that working-class movements are not good because they threaten life-value should be rejected for several reasons.

First, although the idea that unions kill jobs is widely taught in Economics classes, it is not supported even by research done by mainstream economists.[6] Unions push for higher wages. But they also push for shorter hours of work and/or longer paid vacations, gains that increase employment (Jackson 2005: 160).

Second, if a working-class movement is so powerful that some capitalists stop investing in the production of goods and services, it is not inevitable that life-value will be diminished. Strong workers' organizations could pressure the state to step in to provide goods and services people need. Well-organized workers could seize and distribute supplies of vital goods to those who need them. They could also occupy enterprises whose owners have halted production and restart operations under workers' self-management, as has happened in Argentina.[7]

Third, capitalist investment is not a god to which people must bow down. On a global scale, enough wealth and productive capacity already exists to satisfy the physical and socio-cultural life-requirements of every human being.[8] We do not need more. In fact, capitalist economic growth is an underlying cause of the global ecological crisis (Kovel 2007). The problem is not too little capitalist investment but that billions of people are unable to meet their needs while vast amounts of wealth are wasted on military spending, advertising and other expenditures that do no good or actually reduce life-value.

Lastly, if a workers' movement is so strong that some capitalists stop investing and life-value suffers, why should the movement be held responsible rather than the capitalists? Such an "investment strike" is evidence that capitalism causes enormous harm because what matters to it is profit, not human needs (Noonan 2008a).

It is clear that working-class movements can and do have a positive impact on what is good by giving people better access to the means of satisfying their needs and developing their capabilities (this does not mean that everything done by a particular organization or movement contributes to the good — far from it!). To take the case of the movement in Canada and Quebec today, it does raise wages and benefits, defend public services that improve health, have a small positive effect on job security and slightly reduce the weight of oppression. Overall, it does not do much to strengthen social justice struggles or to address the ecological crisis. But a stronger movement would do more to enhance life-value.

The other side of the coin is that if the movement continues to decay, there will be many negative consequences. Some of these will be direct and obvious, such as lower wages, poorer pensions, weaker job security and longer hours in less healthy and less safe workplaces. Other effects will be indirect. These include a weakening of resistance to attacks on public health care, education, water and other public services and even less solidarity among working-class people. Anyone who doubts this need only look at the conditions of work and life in the U.S., where the working-class movement is much weaker than it is north of the border.[9]

Why and How the Movement Needs to Change

Unfortunately, as we have seen, the movement today is showing signs of decay. It gives few workers confidence and hope. It is not organizing the most effective possible resistance to the assault by employers and governments on the working class. Instead, concessions and acceptance of most of what employers and governments are doing is the order of the day. The movement is floundering. As former CAW staffer Sam Gindin has put it,

> We've been under attack for a quarter century now and haven't developed an effective response. That failure is most evident at this moment [of global economic crisis] when, given the exposure of the elite and their governance, they and not us should be on the defensive. (Gindin 2009b: 2)

There is not even much discussion in the movement about the underlying causes of the assault on wages, benefits, rights and public services and how to fight back. As a result, most active union members do not have a clear alternative to the explanations given by employers, politicians and corporate media pundits for what is going on. Other pressing issues of our times and how to address them get even less attention in the unions. These include the ecological crisis, conditions in the Global South, the demands of indigenous people, sexism and racism. Self-critical discussions within the unions about what the movement's problems are and what can be done about them are extremely rare. Few unions are highly democratic. Older white men continue to dominate a multiracial movement in which women outnumber men. Most unions are not doing much to reach out to the non-unionized majority of the working class. Organizations that offer non-unionized workers ways to take collective action to defend themselves or demand more from capitalists or governments — such as workers' centres and groups of unemployed people, tenants, injured workers, poor people, women workers and workers of colour — are few in number and mostly very small. The movement is mostly failing to unite workers across key divisions, such as racism, the gulf between the largely non-unionized private sector and the mostly-unionized public sector, and the split between working-class people with paid work and those who are unwaged. A lot of the movement's political action involves supporting candidates and parties that accept or even push for policies that hurt workers. The movement as it exists today is profoundly inadequate. Workers need and deserve a different, better movement.

That is why the movement needs to change. How should it change? In the broadest terms, it needs to change in ways that help workers address these challenges. The longstanding formula of contract unionism (as the way to deal with workplace concerns) plus voting for "friendly" politicians (as the solution to most other problems) does not help. New methods are needed to build up a greater capacity to fight back. "The problem with unions is not... that they have been too defensive but that in most cases they have not been defensive enough or at least not defensive in a way that allows them to get beyond merely being reactive." What is needed is "a defensiveness that is part of building a culture of resistance" (Panitch and Gindin 2009: 16) among workers. The key changes needed are:

- More democracy. If members do not control their own unions and other organizations, other people whose interests are not the same as theirs — full-time officers and staff or, even worse, employers — will. The power of working-class organizations "lies in the participation of members, and it requires democracy to make members want to be involved" (Parker and Gruelle 1999: 14). Democratically running an organization teaches people new skills and boosts self-confidence. This makes them more likely to use their collective power. A culture in which people are encouraged to speak up, raise tough questions and debate issues in a respectful way is essential in the movement. Mistakes are inevitable, but in democratic organizations, people can learn from mistakes and then make changes

(14–15). The title of Mike Parker and Martha Gruelle's book on changing unions hits the nail on the head: *Democracy is Power*.

- More activists. For the movement to become stronger, it needs more people to become active. Fernando Gapasin, who has been active in movements in the U.S. for many years, believes "there are two keys to developing activism. First, people have to come to the belief that change is necessary and second, that by their action they will contribute to the desired outcome." Effective activists are organizers. They "understand that organizing is about organizing one person at a time. This means organizing people to organize other people" (Gapasin 2009).

- Better activists. As discussed earlier, most union education aims to help workers handle grievances and arbitration cases and negotiate contracts — the stuff of contract unionism. Working-class movement activists, whether they are involved in unions or other organizations, need more than this. Rank-and-file activists need to be able to think and act for themselves, to be less dependent on full-time officers and staff. A lot of what activists need to learn about mobilizing democratically can only come from first-hand experience, through trial and error. Lessons learned through struggles need to be shared. There is also much that cannot be learned just from personal experience (or which is much harder to learn this way), including a basic understanding of how capitalism works, what employers and governments are up to, different forms of oppression and the movement's history. All this calls for a different kind of education for activists than what most union education programs offer.

- Grassroots leadership that reflects the working class. The activist layer in workplaces and neighbourhoods should be as diverse in terms of gender, ethno-racial identity, sexuality and occupation as the actually existing working class in Canada and Quebec.

- More militancy. Militant methods are active and assertive ones, like determined strikes, sit-ins and other kinds of direct action. Militancy is not — contrary to how the term is often used in the corporate media — the same as violence. Militancy refers to the means people use to press for what they want, while radicalism refers to the ends people are trying to achieve.

- More independence. Workers need to become more aware that their interests are different from — and opposed to — the interests of the dominant class. Because their interests are different, workers' organizations should try to be as independent as possible from employers, the legal system and the existing political parties.

- A commitment to mobilizing and organizing the entire working class. As Winnie Ng puts it, "we cannot allow the artificial divide of unionized versus non-unionized workers [to] stop us from re-imagining and re-building a community where no one needs to stand alone: a movement of hope, justice and solidarity" (Ng 2009: 166). A focus only on one's own union, unionized workers, low-income people, wage-earners or any other particular section of the working class is too narrow. The working class is broad, diverse and fragmented. Building a movement of and for all workers should be the aim. This cannot be done through unions alone. Close cooperation between different organizations is called for.

- Deeper and broader solidarity. Because the working class is divided in many ways, solidarity must be actively forged. The old union slogan that "An injury to one is an injury to all" needs to become more than just rhetoric. Some divisions stem mainly from how employment is structured. The split between public and private sector workers is an example. Other divisions are rooted in racism, sexism and other forms of oppression. Workers who belong to groups in society that are privileged rather than oppressed have a special responsibility to extend the hand of solidarity. For example, white workers do not experience racism. To build unity between white workers and people who are directly affected by racism, white people need to educate themselves about racism and challenge it.[10] Building solidarity also involves unionists supporting social justice struggles by people who are not consciously organizing as workers (although most of them probably are part of the working class as understood in this book). Examples include campaigns to reduce greenhouse gas emissions, end violence against women and win permanent resident status for non-status immigrants. Solidarity also needs to extend to struggles against oppression by people who are not part of the working class — for example, indigenous people who live off the land defending their traditional territories from encroachment by corporations. Lastly, solidarity must also be international, in support of people in the U.S. and Mexico and on other continents.
- More radicalism. "The other side has come to understand that... the choices are polarized. To defend their privileges, they've concluded that they must become more radical. We need to learn that same radical lesson, but, of course, from our own perspective" (Gindin 2009b: 2). Being radical does not mean being violent or irrational. It means identifying the root causes of the problems people face (the origin of the word "radical" is the Latin word *radix*, meaning root) and working towards fundamental change in how society is organized.

What these changes add up to is more than a renewal of the movement in its current form. Making these changes would reinvent the working-class movement.

Reinventing the Movement

Reinventing the movement means, quite simply, making sweeping changes in what it does, in how workers are organized and in the way that activists understand the purpose of their organizations and the movement as a whole. Reinvented working-class movement organizations would be ones that workers could use to defend themselves and make gains — in their workplaces and communities — much more effectively than they can today. Making contract unionism more energetic or modifying it is not reinventing the movement. People whose vision goes no further than this are not trying to make the kind of changes just outlined. Recent experience in the U.S. and Canada shows this clearly, as we shall see in the last chapter.

The problem is not that workers are *never* able to use unions as they exist today to defend themselves; this is still possible in unions that are at least slightly democratic. Unions in their current form work — in limited ways — for some workers some of the time. At the most fundamental level, the problem has two sides.

First, unions are becoming less and less effective for the minority of workers who are unionized. What unionized workers are legally allowed to do is constrained by the straightjacket of labour law. The law imposes on unions a narrow focus on representing bargaining unit members in the workplace. The law also pressures officials to act only through collective bargaining, grievances and arbitration. At a time when the balance of power in society is tilting even more in favour of capital, playing by the bureaucratic rules of contract unionism is increasingly ineffective for workers. Moreover, unionism that does little or nothing about issues beyond the workplace fails to address many working-class concerns.

Second, unions are becoming less meaningful for the working class as a whole. The percentage of wage-earners covered by union contracts continues to shrink, especially in the private sector. The union officialdom is increasingly inward-looking. Most of it is preoccupied with administering and negotiating contracts and preserving union institutions, with little time for much more than giving some support to "least bad" politicians at election time. This makes unions less relevant to the many concerns of non-unionized workers, including how to make ends meet; job security; hours of work; health care; pensions; workplace conditions; housing; child care; schools; racist, sexist and heterosexist discrimination and abuse; immigration problems; and the spectre of catastrophic climate change. Tackling both sides of this problem will require nothing short of a reinvention of the movement.

A Look at History

The working-class movement has been reinvented before. The first more or less stable formal workers' movement organizations in the regions of North

America that became Canada in 1867 were craft unions. "Typically a craft union drew its membership from only one occupational group — printers, carpenters, stonemasons, and so on — and admitted only the skilled wage-earners in the trade, the journeymen. Apprentices, women, and unskilled labourers found the union's gates closed to them" (Heron 1996: 6). The strategy of craft unionism was to organize all the members of a particular craft in a locale. If that could be done, craft unionists believed they would be able to compel employers to pay union wage rates and respect their traditional ways of working and the apprenticeship system that limited entry into each craft. Doing this would help preserve their respectability as skilled white men. To complement their unions, many craft unionists became politically active in the Liberal or Conservative parties or, later, moderate "labourist" parties often called Independent Labour Parties. The members of these unions of skilled white male wage-earners did not aspire to unite — each craft had its own separate union. They consciously excluded the vast majority of the working class from their ranks: women, less-skilled workers, indigenous wage-labourers and immigrants from Asia and Eastern Europe (9–18, 31–33, 43–44).

As the development of industrial capitalism reshaped society in the second half of the 1800s, the failings of craft unions became increasingly clear. Their conservative and exclusionary methods offered nothing to most of the working class. They were also being undermined by employers who were introducing machinery operated by less-skilled workers, which reduced capitalists' dependence on skilled craft labour. The first movement organization that represented an alternative to the craft unions on a large scale was the Knights of Labour.[11] This organization — which "combined aspects of a religious brotherhood, a political reform society, a fraternal order, and a pure and simple unionism" (Palmer 1992: 121) flourished for several years in the 1880s. Thousands of workers — men and women of different European heritages (the Knights fully accepted the vicious anti-Asian racism of the time), both skilled and less-skilled — enrolled in the Knights and endorsed their moral vision and rich culture. This was "a process of working-class self-activity that took the collectivist impulses of labouring experience and shaped them into a reform mobilization" (127). But this first effort to reinvent the working-class movement in Canada and Quebec did not last long. By the end of the 1880s, the Knights had faded away, except in Quebec and a few other places where the organization lived on for a while (121–32).

The next effort was rather more successful. The last decade of the 1800s saw the creation of unions whose activists set out to organize wage-earners by industry, not craft. In Canada, industrial unionism first took hold among Western miners. In 1902, the Western Federation of Miners (WFM), with members on both sides of the Canada-U.S. border, launched the American

Labor Union (ALU) as an alternative to the central labour bodies of the craft unions, the American Federation of Labour and its Canadian counterpart, the Trades and Labour Congress. ALU unionists were committed to organizing any and all wage-workers and declared the ALU for socialism. The ALU had a presence in Canada as well as the U.S. In 1905, the membership of the ALU merged with other like-minded unionists to create the Industrial Workers of the World (IWW). The hallmarks of the IWW's unionism were militant direct action; democratic control of the organization by its members; working-class solidarity across all divisions, including "race"; a lively down-to-earth multilingual culture of less-skilled and mostly male wage-earners; and the aim of replacing capitalism with a society run by working people. Other industrial unions less radical than the IWW were also created, though their activists were generally socialists of some kind. Many industrial unionists were involved in the socialist groups and parties that were formed in the same period. These offered workers left-wing political alternatives (Heron 1996: 35–42; Leier 1990).

Industrial unions and socialist organizations together represented a reinvention of the working-class movement. This reinvention took place not only in Canada and the U.S. but also in other advanced capitalist countries (Peterson 1981). These new organizations were dramatically different from craft unionism and labourism (which continued to exist, their leaders often bitterly hostile to what they saw as illegitimate upstart organizations of the rabble). Industrial unionists faced stiff opposition and sometimes intimidation and violence from employers and state authorities. But workers were better able to fight for what they needed through the new organizations than through those that had developed decades earlier. The new ways of organizing were simply better suited to the conditions of industrial capitalism than those of craft unionism. A century later, the reinvention the movement needs in order to respond much more effectively to contemporary capitalism will have to involve forms of action and organization that are as different from those that are most common in the movement today as the IWW's were from the methods of the craft unions.[12]

Can It Be Done Again?

But is such a reinvention possible in the twenty-first century? There is no doubt there are major obstacles to the development of different working-class movement organizations in Canada and Quebec. The weakness of the infrastructure of dissent is one of these. Figuring out new ways to organize requires "the means of analysis, communication, organization and sustenance that nurture the capacity for collective action" (Sears 2005: 32). As we have seen in Chapter Six, these were significant a century ago, but are often missing today. The weakness of the infrastructure of dissent is one of the reasons why there are so few supporters of radical left-wing politics in the workers' movement. In the late 1800s and early 1900s, "socialists were the foremost advocates of industrial unionism and leaders of the new unions" (Heron 1996: 36); today, there are very few radicals active in unions, and only slightly more in other working-class movement groups. As a result, many workers who sense some of the limitations of unions and the NDP have never encountered a clear analysis of these problems and alternative ideas about what to do. People who do understand many of the shortcomings of the movement in its present form and want to do something about them are often isolated from like-minded activists in other union locals, community-based groups and regions.

Another obstacle is the weakening of ties among people in the places where they work for wages:

> As a result of new technologies and the reorganization of work (in-cluding speed-up, downsizing, standardization, and job combination, as well as formal restructuring programs such as lean, kaizen, Six Sigma, and the Toyota Production System) workers are increasingly working alone, isolated from their co-workers. This isolation, in turn, hinders the formation of "dense networks of interconnection." (Richardson 2008: 70)

Ties among wage-earners on the job are especially significant because con-nections outside the workplace are usually even weaker (there are exceptions, such as workplaces where coworkers have close ties to each other off the job because they belong to the same ethno-racial or religious community).

A third obstacle is the way that labour law imposes obligations and restrictions on certified unions. These impositions foster "responsible" contract unionism. This is an obstacle that early industrial unionists did not face (they had to deal with being denied employment, beaten up or worse, but not laws designed to shape unions in this narrow way). It means that creating new and more effective unions, as groups of workers have done in a few countries, including France and New Zealand in the late twentieth century, and industrial unionists did a century earlier, would not be an escape from one of the forces that have made unions in Canada and Quebec what they are today.[13] Another legal issue is that labour law in Canada and Quebec gives no rights to unions that have not been certified as the bargaining agent for a unit of employees. This means there is no legal protection or status for unions made up of a minority of workers in a workplace, which is what many early industrial union activists built as a step towards a union with enough support that the employer would be forced to recognize it and negotiate with union representatives.

These are real obstacles. They help explain why there has been so little activity of the kind that could reinvent the movement in response to the challenges of neoliberal capitalism. Nevertheless, it would be a serious mistake to leap from that to the conclusion that the working-class movement *cannot* be reinvented. The movement has been written off before, only to defy predictions. Its history reveals that workers' resistance ebbs and flows, and the ways workers organize change, yet working-class resistance and organization is never entirely extinguished (Mason 2008). What the belief that the movement cannot be reinvented does do, unfortunately, is make people think that unions practicing "responsible" contract unionism is all the movement can ever be. This discourages people from trying to organize in different and more effective ways.

Studying the history of capitalism and how capitalism works as a system does allow us to be certain about some things. One is that whatever workers have — income, benefits, housing, pensions, health care, rights and more — is never safe from attack by employers, bankers and governments, as many people in rich countries who thought they were secure have learned from the Great Recession and the new wave of austerity policies that governments are implementing. Another is that capitalism's drive for profit poses a permanent threat to human life-value (Noonan 2008a; McNally 2006). The global ecological crisis created by capitalism has raised this threat to a new level (Kovel 2007). Understanding these things brings us back to the heart of the matter: a stronger working-class movement would be a good thing, and the movement in Canada and Quebec needs to be reinvented. The odds of this happening cannot be known, but the goal is worthy. If the movement needs to be reinvented, the crucial question is how can people work to make real change happen?

Notes

1. In other words, have too few members of colour, especially in leadership positions at all levels.
2. Time devoted to unpaid domestic work is not experienced as "an open matrix of human possibilities." In addition, in out society, much of people's time outside the hours spent working for pay is organized by the "leisure/consumer/entertainment industries" into modules, each of which involves consuming different commodities (Noonan 2009: 10). As a result, for many people, "the experience of empty time appears as a burden to be filled through some commodified form of activity" (11).
3. Michael Moore's film *Capitalism: A Love Story* (2009) includes a scene of activists associated with the Miami Workers' Centre preventing a family from being made homeless in Florida.
4. On how liberal democracy is a democracy that has been greatly diluted by capitalism, see McNally 2006: 268–76.
5. On the potential transformative power of workers' movements, see McNally 2006: 369–78. Noonan 2008c makes a compelling life-grounded case for why capitalism should be replaced by socialism (by which he means socialist democracy, not a bureaucratic dictatorship).

6. Mainstream economists accept the right-wing dogmas that dominate their discipline. For a critical look at these dogmas, see Yates 2003: 119–56.
7. On worker-run enterprises in Argentina, see Lavaca 2007 and the movie *The Take* (Lewis 2004).
8. One need only compare the spending required to meet the modest UN Millennium Development Goals <undp.org/mdg> with global military spending (see the documentation of the Stockholm International Peace Research Institute at <sipri. org>) to see this. Not all physical and socio-cultural life-requirements require many resources to satisfy — consider the needs for physical activity and play, for example.
9. For an introduction to conditions in the U.S., see <stateofworkingamerica.org>.
10. On white people and anti-racism in Canada, see Wilmot 2005.
11. In Nova Scotia, the Provincial Workmen's Association organized coal miners and a few other groups of skilled wage-earners (Heron 1996: 19).
12. Some have argued that the historical analogy for what the movement needs today is not early twentieth century radical industrial unionism's challenge to craft unionism but the rise of the industrial unions of the CIO in the 1930s and 1940s. While the union breakthrough of those decades was undoubtedly a great step forward for the working class, CIO-style industrial unionism was much less democratic, militant and radical than earlier industrial unions like the IWW, the One Big Union and the unions of the Workers' Unity League (including its organizations of the unemployed). Most CIO leaders supported "responsible" bureaucratic contract unionism (Davis 1986: 55–62; Lynd 1992: 30–31; Heron 1996: 57, 62–63, 70–71). The widespread establishment of this kind of unionism, discussed in Chapter Six, certainly transformed unions in Canada and Quebec and improved workers' lives. But this was not a reinvention of the movement in a dramatically new form that was *much* more effective for the working class, as earlier industrial unionism and, for a short time, the Knights of Labour had been.
13. For a brief introduction to the Solidaires union in France, see Baron 2009. On New Zealand's Unite, see Annis 2009. In the 1960s and 1970s, militant union members in some U.S.-headquartered CLC-affiliated unions split away to form independent Canadian unions affiliated to the Confederation of Canadian Unions, which by 2008 had dwindled away to fewer than 8000 members. Canadian feminist activists also formed the Service, Office and Retail Workers Union of Canada (SORWUC) as a union outside the CLC in 1972, "with a primary goal to organize women in industries neglected by trade unions" (Nicol 1997: 236). SORWUC folded in 1986.

8. How to Reinvent the Movement?

If a stronger working-class movement is a worthy goal, and the movement needs to be reinvented in order to become much stronger, we face the question of how can people begin to make this kind of change happen? Most advocates of changing the movement in order to strengthen it argue for a version of "reform from above," to use Moody's term (2007). This chapter begins by examining this approach and the most important recent attempts to put it into practice in Canada. Many supporters of reform from above believe in corporate unionism; others see mobilization unionism as the direction in which the movement should go. Although practicing mobilization unionism can bring about some progressive changes, no version of reform from above is a road to the kind of far-reaching change needed in the movement. What does have potential to reinvent the movement is a very different approach: working to reform unions from below and also build new workers' organizations. After outlining this alternative approach, the chapter surveys some examples of activity that should give hope to people who want to try to change the movement from below. Finally, the question of how people committed to reinventing the movement should deal with politics is examined.

Reform from Above

Most discussions about changing the movement in Canada and Quebec have been influenced by developments in U.S. unions. In 1995, the New Voice slate headed by John Sweeney, president of the SEIU, defeated AFL-CIO Secretary-Treasurer Tom Donahue and his allies in a contest for the top positions in the U.S. union federation. This move was a response from within the very highest ranks of the labour officialdom to the accelerating decline of U.S. union membership, density and influence on governments. The Sweeney leadership team launched a number of campaigns and initiatives that aimed to raise union density and elect more Democratic Party politicians. These included recruiting and training hundreds of university students to become union organizers and trying to build up local labour councils in alliance with community organizations (Moody 2007: 125–37; Fletcher and Gapasin 2008: 69–82). The changes at the top of the AFL-CIO certainly "created hope" (70) among union and social justice activists in the U.S. and beyond. Much of this hope evaporated in the years that followed as the limitations of the new leaders and their program became evident (Moody 2007: 133–42; Fletcher and Gapasin 2008: 70–86, 100–20).

Change was not limited to what was happening at the AFL-CIO. A number of U.S.-headquartered unions — above all, SEIU, HERE and UNITE — were reorganizing and putting a lot of resources into energetic and strategically planned drives to sign up thousands of new members in private and public sector service jobs, many of them women, immigrants and/or workers of colour (Moody 2007: 184–88). Most of the top leaders of these unions were also committing more money and staff to elect Democrats and support community allies. Their paramount goal was to raise union density in the industries and sectors within industries that they chose to target. As a key SEIU staffer put it, unions had to boost up their "market share" (Early 2009: 212). SEIU officials embraced partnerships with employers in exchange for winning collective agreement coverage for the employees of these firms. In 2005, SEIU, UNITE HERE, UFCW and four other unions quit the AFL-CIO and launched another federation, Change to Win. This move drew more attention to these "organizing" unions.[1]

All these developments led to a lot of talk about "union renewal" among academics sympathetic to unions. They also had echoes in Canada (and, to a lesser extent, in Quebec). Many activists and academics in Canada who want to see stronger unions have been inspired in one way or another by the approach taken by the top leaders of unions like SEIU and UNITE HERE. Most people who talk about union renewal have been influenced by it. But what is this approach? What kind of change does it envision for unions?

"Union renewal" can mean many things. Every kind of unionism can be given new life; almost any union's approach can be presented as an example of renewal.[2] That said, most people in Canada who want unions to become stronger and most people who talk about union renewal share a common theme. Their visions of how unions should change are visions of reform from above. This approach can be appealing for activists who are frustrated with the difficulty of convincing other workers to mobilize collectively and draw the conclusion that "by ascending the union ladder, they will acquire more power to 'educate' the members around them."[3]

In the reform from above approach, the key players are union officials. In order to move forward, a union needs a central team of talented top officers and staff that can come up with strategic plans and the money needed to pay for new campaigns. These top leaders must also have the authority to ensure that the officers, staff and active members at lower levels of the union "stay on program." To carry out the program, unions must "staff up" — hire more organizers, researchers and other staff. Staffers must be willing to dedicate themselves to the cause and carry out orders from the top in a disciplined way. The ability to mobilize members — whether on picket lines, in the streets, at the ballot box at election time or even on the job — is usually seen as vital because it gives officials bargaining clout when dealing with employers and politicians. As the Action Agenda circulated by leaders of the TYRLC before the 2008 CLC convention put it, "Canada's labour movement has... the vision, but not the power, to shape the political agenda.... Our challenge, put bluntly, is how we build that power." One of the keys, the Action Agenda said, was "the engagement of members and allies in grass-roots mobilization in both the workplace and the community."[4] But for supporters of reform from above the important decisions about when and how to mobilize are to be made by officials, not democratically by workers themselves (Moody 2007: 173–96; Abott-Klofter et al. 2009; Early 2009: 209–24).

Supporters of change through reform from above often want to see local labour councils, provincial federations of labour and the CLC become more centralized organizations under dynamic leaders with the power to marshal people and money for strategic campaigns. Such a vision was spelled out in the TYRLC's Action Agenda.[5] Specifically, this called on the CLC to campaign for changes to labour law that would allow workers in every province to certify a union when a majority of the would-be bargaining unit members sign union membership cards, without having to hold a vote (card-check certification); set up a task force on union organizing; challenge precarious employment, "unfair trade deals" and privatization; work to raise provincial minimum wages; develop a "green jobs" strategy; promote equity within unions; "call for an end to the war in Afghanistan" and "educate Canadians about the war"; strengthen labour councils; and push governments to purchase goods made in Canada.

Thinking back to the varieties of unionism discussed earlier, what kind of unionism is being promoted by advocates of reform from above? Many are pushing for corporate unionism, the "union density at all costs" approach that dominates in SEIU and UNITE HERE.[6] A minority favour mobilization unionism.[7] These varieties of unionism are different in important ways. Mobilization unionism involves a serious commitment to fighting for social justice, not just raising union density. Its supporters are more critical of employers and right-wing governments. Nevertheless, in practice, supporters of both mobilization unionism and corporate unionism look to enlightened full-time union officers and staff as the key to changing unions and building union power. Promoters of corporate unionism are hostile to efforts to make unions more democratic (Moody 2007: 176–79, 194; Early 2009: 226–30, 251–55; Abott-Klofter et al. 2009). Mobilization unionists at their best treat union democracy as not very important (Downs 2006). At worst, as in the CAW in the second half of the 1990s, they oppose greater membership control.

The TYRLC is currently the most visible organization in Canada identified with pushing for change in the movement. Under the leadership of John Cartwright, Toronto's labour council has turned in the direction of mobilization unionism, as is clear from its actions and publications.[8] The

TYRLC has few full-time officials of its own and relatively little money. Its leaders must rely on the efforts of officials and rank-and-file activists from the union locals affiliated to it in order to carry out council activities. Nevertheless, since the middle of the first decade of the twenty-first century, the TYRLC has developed a high profile both in and beyond Canada's largest city.

There are three main reasons why the TYRLC has caught the attention of so many labour activists. The first is that no other leadership of a union organization has responded to the situation the movement finds itself in by proposing a clear strategic direction and agenda for change for unions as a whole. Second, anti-racism and building alliances between unions and community organizations have been central to the TYRLC leadership's project. Third, TYRLC officials have organized well-attended events and done a good job of publicizing them after the fact as well as when motivating people to attend.[9]

The most-noticed one of these events was probably the May 2009 Stewards Assembly, which drew as many as 1600 union stewards and other officers, activists and staff to a large downtown hotel for an evening of "'We can do it!'-style rallying cries" (Anonymous 2009) in speeches and presentations. CAW economist Jim Stanford's explanation of the economic crisis was followed by "pre-arranged interventions from the floor, mostly by workers of colour who are struggling, with some limited successes, in the current crisis" (Anonymous 2009). The evening was heralded "in TYRLC communications to affiliated unions since the end of March as... an 'historic event' needed to develop a 'collective response' to the economic crisis" (Anonymous 2009). Cartwright hailed the assembly in the same way in the full-colour magazine-format publication about the event that was published soon afterwards (TYRLC 2009b). Former CAW staffer Herman Rosenfeld (2009a: 37–38) was more measured, noting it was "the first such meeting in living memory" and "the result of an impressive organizing effort." Yet "rather than being an actual assembly, with open discussion, debate and space for the stewards to initiate points and ideas, it felt more like a process of conveying information." There were "constant references to NDP politicians" and the evening ended with a speech by Mayor David Miller (at the time, the negotiations that would soon push CUPE Locals 79 and 416 on strike were taking place and major demands for concessions from the City of Toronto's unions were on the table).

The TYRLC leadership's project involves a lot of emphasis on "political bargaining" — in other words, lobbying politicians — and other kinds of parliamentary political action around all levels of government. This is combined with building alliances with community groups, particularly those based in communities of colour. For example, the TYRLC's leaders directed a 2007 campaign to raise Ontario's minimum wage that combined print and online petitions with "the holding of community-based meetings in various racially-diverse, lower income neighbourhoods" (Wilmot 2008a: 18) in support of an NDP MPP's private member's bill. The council's Labour Education Centre (LEC) offers not only "tools" courses, but also courses such as "Migrant Workers in a Global Economy" and "Organizing Across Boundaries: Class, Race and Culture." Leadership Institutes have also been held. The TYRLC's top leaders have made a conscious effort over a number of years to increase the representation of people of colour as delegates to the council and members of its executive. Annual Aboriginal/Workers of Colour conferences have been geared to this goal. The effort has succeeded in increasing the number of people of colour who are delegates, officers and staff of the TYRLC.[10]

The key question that needs to be asked about the approach of trying to change the movement through reform from above is simple: how well can it bring about the changes that the movement needs in order to respond to the challenges it faces? To be fair, we should deal with corporate unionism separately from mobilization unionism.

Corporate unionism, with its single-minded focus on bringing more workers under collective agreements, does not even involve trying to make most of the changes that are needed. At its best, as in parts of UNITE HERE, practicing corporate unionism can encourage union members to become active and foster solidarity among workers (Abbott-Klafter et al. 2009; Tufts 2006). However, its supporters do not necessarily try to achieve even these changes. This is obvious in SEIU, in which "exchanging stewards for call centers" (Abbott-Klafter et al. 2009) is now part of the program and members often have, in the words of a former SEIU organizer in Ontario, "no input into the direction"(G 2007: 17) of the local union. Staff-driven unions in which decisions are made at the top of a highly centralized officialdom are the opposite of democratic workers' organizations. Mobilizing workers to participate in union actions that are planned, led or cancelled by full-time officials must not be confused with democracy.[11] Partnership deals with employers that get unions more members but bind unions to bosses' goals and schemes — such as those signed by SEIU officials in the health care sector in the U.S. (Early 2009: 235–36) and by the CAW brass with Magna — tie workers to capitalists rather than building workers' independence. When supporters of corporate unionism succeed in bringing wage-earners union representation, what workers gain is only "a shallow kind of power resting on staff and long contracts" (Moody 2007: 194). This "'density without democracy' is a deficiency that can, over time, seriously undermine union contract enforcement and rank-and-file militancy on the job" (Early 2009: 213). A widespread turn to corporate unionism in Canada and Quebec would probably raise union density somewhat, but what kind of organizations would be growing? The bolstered ranks of labour would belong to unions that workers would have great difficulty using as organizations for collective action in their own interests. Such unions perpetuate ways of acting and thinking that have contributed to the process of decay in the working-class movement. Corporate unionism is clearly not the answer.

What about the version of reform from above that promotes mobilization unionism? The CAW during the second half of the 1990s and the TYRLC today are the most important recent Canadian examples of labour organizations whose leading officials have endorsed this approach and put it into practice. As mentioned earlier, the CAW's top officials began to move to the right and away from their experiments with mobilization unionism after the end of the Ontario Days of Action in 1999. This move quickened under the influence of the right-wing political fallout of 9/11 and the CAW officialdom cozying up with employers at the "Big Three" unionized auto companies that faced growing competition from non-unionized Toyota and Honda (Allen 2006). The fact that there was only minimal opposition within the CAW to this shift to the right shows just how important a genuine culture of democracy is to making lasting progressive change in the working-class movement. If membership control is weak, changes can easily be reversed when official leaders decide to steer in a different direction. Such a culture of democracy never existed in the CAW. Its top leaders never stopped using their Administration Caucus to exercise tight control. The "follow the leader" attitudes they fostered among staff, elected officers and the rank-and-file membership by running the union in the manner they had learned in the Bob White School of Obedience were never seriously challenged. Once Buzz Hargrove and other top leaders began moving right, a number of positive changes that had taken place in the CAW in the 1990s were lost. Official CAW support for politics to the left of the NDP was shed, along with backing for extra-parliamentary struggles by unions and global justice and anti-poverty groups. Any effort to be independent from all of the major political parties was jettisoned. The CAW's extensive education program remained, along with other mechanisms to encourage members to become union activists and to develop workers of colour and women as leaders. However, these were no longer part of any effort to remake the CAW and change the union movement.

Looking at the TYRLC also helps evaluate the potential of mobilization unionism. The work of its officers and staff has undoubtedly built up activism in the council. The TYRLC's activists and staff have become more multiracial, closer to mirroring Toronto's working class in the early twenty-first century. Some of the LEC's courses aim to make better activists and foster solidarity. Joint activity with community groups, including the Good Jobs Coalition,[12] points unionists beyond a narrow focus on the workplace problems of unionized workers and beyond charity. University and college student unions belonging to the Canadian Federation of Students can now affiliate to the TYRLC.[13] Since most students are non-unionized wage-earners, this is a little step towards broadening the council beyond the members of CLC-affiliated unions. These are all progressive changes. Few other labour organizations have done as well or better in recent years.

But the project of the TYRLC's leaders does not address other vital changes that need to happen. Above all, making unions more democratic is not part of their agenda. There is not one word in TYRLC publications about democratic change within unions — a taboo idea in the upper reaches of the union officialdom and most of its lower echelons, too. The delegates from affiliated unions who attend monthly TYRLC meetings do not exercise a lot of control over the activities of the council. Nor has the TYRLC leadership tried to move unions in a more radical direction. The council's 2004–10 strategy document predicted that "across the world... workers will find new forms of solidarity in the struggle against global capitalism" (TYRLC n.d. [2004]: 2), but the actions of the TYRLC have not been guided by any politics of anti-capitalist struggle.[14] The TYRLC was tightly linked with Mayor David Miller and his allies on Toronto's city council, who were hardly independent of business.[15] The basis for this relationship has been "a modest political program that rests on lower business taxes and co-operation between labour and private investors." It should have been no surprise, then, that the hundreds of people who attended the May 2009 Stewards Assembly were given a picture of the global economic crisis whose "critique of the financial sector was limited to complaints about speculation and excess profits" with "no mention of... reforms such as nationalizing the banks" (Rosenfeld 2009a: 38) and no critique of capitalism itself.[16] Yet even if the TYRLC leadership were to move in a more radical direction, the stage would be set for a move away from radicalism as seen in the CAW, unless the council were to become much more democratic. The history of workers' movements shows that the radicalism of full-time officers and staff is usually trumped by the pressures that come from being part of the bureaucratic labour officialdom; being accountable to an organized base of radical workers is a counterweight to these pressures.[17] Another problem with the TYRLC has been a pattern of organizing from event to event, including large union-community conferences and the Stewards Assembly, in a way that does not build the movement or engage in specific struggles. A USW activist who sees the TYRLC as an "area of hope" nevertheless described the pattern of going from event to event this way: "You march people up to the top of the hill and you march them down again and you say, 'Wow, isn't that wonderful? See how many people were at the top of the hill.'"[18]

The TYRLC today, like the CAW experience, reveals that practicing mobi-lization unionism can do more for the movement than corporate unionism.

However, even a more consistent adoption of mobilization unionism is not a good enough way of working towards the kinds of change that need to happen in the working-class movement. Neither variant of the reform from above approach involves people trying to make the truly thorough change the movement's current situation calls for. If reform from above is not the road to reinventing the movement, what is?

Reform from Below and Building New Organizations

At the heart of this alternative approach is a simple idea: workers themselves are the key players in changing the working-class movement. People should try to change unions and other labour bodies by working from the inside and from the bottom up to promote democracy, militancy and solidarity. The emphasis is on activism where the largest number of wage-earners can get involved and where they have the most potential power: in the workplace and at the level of the local union. This grassroots emphasis goes along with a vision of building a fighting movement of the working class for social change.

To achieve such a movement, divisions among workers need to be challenged. Separate organizing by what are sometimes called "equity-seeking" groups (people who face oppression) — women, people of colour, LGBT workers, indigenous people and people with disabilities — and joint efforts by members of these groups can be a useful tactic for building support for action against oppression (Briskin 2009).

Union activists committed to the from below approach should, wherever possible, form their own independent groupings of like-minded people (such as caucuses or networks) to organize their efforts. Efforts to change unions from below are essential. So, too, are campaigns to help more wage-earners form unions.

Yet these are not enough. The movement needs to take up all the concerns of working-class people, on or off the job: "If you're going to build solidarity you have to be relevant to people as a *whole*, because you can't split up people's lives."[19] When union activists get their organizations to start taking action on issues outside the workplace, they sometimes discover there are members who had not been active in the union before who care about these issues and are willing to get involved. This can strengthen a union's activist base.[20] However, even the best unions cannot possibly take on every struggle facing the entire working class, so creating other organizations to mobilize people around issues affecting them is also important (this was understood by activists in Quebec's CSN when they called for a "Second Front" in 1968 [Mills 2010: 165]). These organizations can come in many forms. Workers' centres, neighbourhood associations in lower-income areas, groups of tenants or unemployed people and groups that focus on anti-racism and the rights of migrants are only some of the possibilities.

From this perspective, unions and such organizations really are all part of the same movement and should work together. The aim is to work to overcome the separation of "labour" and "community" by promoting unity and solidarity among the various organizations of the working class. Together, rebel-led union locals, groups of members in other unions who are committed to social movement unionism and other activist organizations could begin to "put the movement back into the movement," to use a catch-phrase of the U.S. publication *Labor Notes*. Why is this approach a road to reinventing the movement? Quite simply because it tries to make the full range of changes that were identified in the last chapter as necessary to respond to the actual challenges the movement faces (not only those changes that are acceptable to the more militant upper-level union officials).

As argued in the previous chapter, democracy is tremendously important. This is understood by people who support this alternative approach. Active members who really do democratically control the organization and try to get others to become involved are key to building workers' power, whether in a union local or another kind of group. Democratic involvement — as opposed to participation in activities planned and prepared by others — can have a real impact on people. As a former rank-and-file auto worker activist puts it, a democratic "opening up... is not something that is going to change things overnight." But it "changes the way people think... about their own union... [by] start[ing] to think about it as their own." Also, "once they actually participate in it and have a stake in it they talk about it differently in their communities and in their neighbourhoods. So that changes the culture of how people talk about unions." Greater democracy also makes it harder for anyone to use the union "for personal gain."[21] Activists who truly understand why genuine democracy is so important will not make the mistake of using undemocratic methods in trying to make change in the movement. They will recognize, for example, why involving lots of members in a process of education, discussion and debate before making a decision on a controversial issue is much better than rushing to get a motion passed at a poorly-attended membership meeting. It is not just the decision that matters, but how the decision is reached and who takes part in making it.

Increasing democracy improves workers' capacity to organize themselves (rather than being organized by union officials or others acting on their behalf) and to engage in direct action. As a former CAW staffer says,

> part of the problem now is that workers need some confidence so they can do things other than sit home or just trust someone else to do things for them. Because [most] people don't have an immediate experience of collective action winning things for them.[22]

A more democratic organization makes it easier for people to feel they can act collectively. "When the members run the union, they have chances to measure their collective strength against the boss, and gain the confidence to use it" (Parker and Gruelle 1999: 14). This can start in very small ways:

> When members, for instance, see that a cartoon they've posted on the union bulletin board really shakes up the supervisor, they start thinking about other ways to push that boss's discomfort into positive changes (and they think up more cartoon ideas). Yet many unions keep their bulletin boards behind locked glass. (14)

On a much larger scale, workers in a highly democratic union are more likely to fight to win — defying the law if necessary — than workers in a union controlled by full-time officials who are preoccupied with the union as an institution and worry a lot about fines and other possible consequences. The picture is similar for organizations other than unions. For example, a grassroots anti-poverty group run democratically by low-income people is more likely to engage in self-organized direct action, such as occupying the office of a government ministry to demand improvements for people on social assistance, than one that is dependent on government or foundation funding and run by paid staff.

From the perspective of this bottom-up worker-driven approach, the role of full-time union officers and staff and their counterparts in community organizations should be to assist workers to build member-run democratic organizations. Full-timers who support this approach to changing the movement should always strive to help workers develop their capacities. This means taking care to not substitute their own efforts, no matter how well-intentioned, for those of the rank-and-file. For example, a union official can prepare a group of workers to challenge an abusive manager themselves rather than do so on their behalf. The ultimate aim of full-timers should be to make themselves unnecessary.[23] Most experienced activists who support this approach are well aware that *very* few full-time union officers and staff in Canada and Quebec try to act in this way.[24]

Supporters of this approach have different ideas about what leadership means. Some treat leadership as a matter of abilities and skills that should be developed among as many workers as possible. From this viewpoint, activists should try to foster new leaders. Others see leadership as a problem to be done away with. A related issue, on which there are different views, is when (or if) supporters of changing the movement from below should run for union office (full-time or otherwise) or take staff jobs.[25]

Putting the Approach into Practice
How can this approach be put into practice within existing unions? Crucially, the starting point is *not* the strategic vision of working to reinvent the move-

ment that has just been outlined. To start here would be a recipe for failure, since so few people consciously endorse it today. People with this vision need to remember the basic truth expressed by a CAW activist: "Groups that make themselves relevant by directly impacting the day to day lives of the people they need to mobilize are by far the most successful at challenging the status quo and creating real social change" (Johnston 2008: 50). In unions, this means that workers' concerns and "actually existing worker resistance" (Cohen 2006: 172) are where to begin.

In workplaces in a capitalist society, there are always issues that concern workers. There is no substitute for workplace action around issues that matter to people where they work for pay.[26] Union issues can be brought up in the workplace: "The broadest, and often the most honest and imaginative, discussions about union strategies happen informally at work — on breaks or at lunch, or waiting for the copier" (Parker and Gruelle 1999: 39). Opportunities to challenge the bureaucracy of contracts, law and restrictive union rules need to be seized when they arise, no matter how small they are. This usually involves direct action, "that is, taking action ourselves rather than waiting for others to solve the problem" (Slaughter 2005: 9).Workplace agitation comes in many forms, from a group of members presenting a grievance together to challenging harassment collectively to brief work stoppages to more militant actions, such as the walk out at Vancouver General Hospital reported in Chapter One or workers "locking out the boss" at a Toronto postal station (23–25). Contract campaigns that mobilize workers in the fight for better collective agreements are important, as are strikes. So, too, is extra-parliamentary political action, especially demonstrations and marches that are not just token affairs. Union activism of this kind nurtures solidarity, self-organization and the confidence to take collective action. The experience of collective action changes people, especially (but not only) when the action is successful. It gives workers a sense of their power. It opens people up to ideas about the possibility of making change they previously thought made no sense. That is why the "strategic, conscious building of rank-and-file organisation and resistance" (Cohen 2006: 182) is so important.

Members care more about the union when unionism means coworkers tackling their problems together rather than just dues deducted from pay-cheques. When this happens, members are much more likely to go to union meetings and get involved in changing their unions. Union activism that builds workplace power also opens the door to unionized workers becoming active around issues that are not directly related to their workplaces or that they thought did not concern them — a vital feature of social movement unionism. The reflections of a CAW activist are worth quoting at length:

Workplace success is what enables broader social struggle. The union must be relevant and effective in improving working conditions before its members will believe in it as a vehicle for social reform. We must be able to mobilize workers in the workplace in order to be able to mobilize them on social issues. It's not that social issues and struggle aren't important to workers, but rather that workplace resistance is prerequisite to social success.

You can't expect a worker to care about injustice in the community and then tell him the injustice they see their co-worker face is just the way the system works. How can you expect workers to have the confidence to take on complex social issues if they're told that they're not qualified to handle what they know best, workplace issues? How do you build the faith that a better world is possible when unions are telling workers that concessions are necessary for their survival? (Johnston 2008: 12)

An example of successful struggle with an employer powering mobilization outside the workplace was the way that CUPE Local 3903's January 2001 strike victory (Kuhling 2002) fueled members' participation in the protests against the summit negotiating a Free Trade Area of the Americas in Quebec City in April that year. Inspiration can also move in the opposite direction: experiences of struggle outside the workplace can feed back into challenges to employers. For instance, OCAP's militant June 15, 2000, march on the provincial legislature in Toronto, where marchers were attacked by police and many fought back (McNally 2000), influenced people who were soon to be active in CUPE 3903's strike.[27] Global justice protests in Seattle (1999), Washington (2000) and Windsor (2000) did the same (Kuhling 2002: 80).

Independent initiatives by activists — outside the official structures of the unions — are an essential tactic for putting social movement unionism into practice. A newsletter can be an organizing tool. Newsletters can help activists communicate their ideas to coworkers, organize campaigns and help like-minded people connect with each other. They are especially important in undemocratic locals where it is hard for opponents of the official leaders to present their dissenting ideas to members. By forming caucuses, committees or other groupings, members who share a common approach can work together to advance their proposals for change. Such groupings are useful when running candidates for union office. When they are strong enough, they can also organize actions independently of officials when necessary (Slaughter 2005: 26–28, 272–81). In some cases, they provide important links between people in different work sites and union locals.

Independent organization can take different forms. For example, workers at Toronto's Metropolitan Hotel formed a rank-and-file committee in response to the inaction of officers and staff of HERE Local 75 (Tang

2004). In contrast, after the defeat of HEU's 2004 strike a Solidarity Caucus was launched by members of different B.C. unions who supported social movement unionism. Its statement of purpose declared, "It's Time to Start Changing Our Unions."[28] The flying squads formed early in the first decade of the twenty-first century by members of a number of locals to support others' struggles during the heyday of the global justice movement showed a different path to workers' independent organizing.[29] What these three examples have in common is that they were all groups of unionized workers coming together outside official structures in order to do things that could not be done through those bureaucratic channels.

Because social movement unionism is about building a *class-wide* movement, bodies that bring together members of locals of the same union or, better yet, different unions are valuable. The most common such organization is a labour council made up of representatives from CLC-affiliated unions in a region (Quebec's CSN federation also has regional councils). In some unions, there are also bodies composed of delegates from its locals within a region, such as the CUPE district councils that exist in some cities. Labour councils today are only bodies of delegates from locals affiliated to a labour federation, and are sometimes dominated by full-time officials. However, making them more democratic and opening them up to representatives of other movement groups where these exist would make them closer to being local class-wide organizations. In the same spirit, coalitions that unite union activists with activists from other social justice groups provide opportunities to build solidarity on a broader basis. So, too, do grassroots international workers' solidarity projects (Moody 1997: 249–68). Simply bringing different groups of people together in solidarity — such as when students walk on picket lines with striking unionists, public and private sector workers support each other or well-paid union members take part in anti-poverty actions with low-income people — is always worthwhile.

This look at putting the reform from below approach into practice would not be complete without a mention of organizing more non-unionized workers into unions. The democratic and bottom-up perspective on union organizing is the opposite of the corporate unionist willingness to do just about anything to get more workers covered by collective agreements, including trading away the right to strike, stewards in the workplace and any semblance of democratic organization. Instead of tightly staff-run "drive by organizing" that treats getting a first contract as the end of the story, social movement unionists put workers organizing themselves at the centre of efforts to expand union membership. This means, for example, building a strong committee of pro-union workers who begin to act like union activists and can make decisions during an organizing campaign instead of just carrying out decisions made by union staff. Participants in a workshop on organizing at a 1998 CLC women's symposium identified four principles that fit with this approach:

- Workers need unions! Workers are the union. The union must reflect the workers.
- Act like a union — always.
- Look for and develop internal leaders from the very beginning and throughout the campaign, up to and including negotiating the first contract.
- A union's role is to reduce competition among workers which always allows the boss to win. We need to reduce competition among unions, for the same reason. (CLC 1998: 8–9)

Having volunteer organizers who are rank-and-file union members from workplaces similar to the one where the campaign is taking place makes union organizing more of a worker-to-worker process. The women at the 1998 CLC workshop also clearly spelled out another way of making organizing more effective:

> Include community members in organizing drives as full participants. Many community groups and individuals support unions and will volunteer to help, to provide language translation and reassurances that can counteract anti-union propaganda. Community activists can also help overcome cultural and community practices: for example, how do you stand up to elders who may be opposed to unions, when your cultural traditions demand you respect the views of your elders? (10)

Taking this approach integrates lessons learned by unionists who have experience organizing in immigrant communities. Broadening out who is included in an organizing drive makes union-building a step closer to becoming a class-wide concern, not something that only matters for the potential union members. When a campaign by democratically self-organized workers and their allies to create a new union succeeds, there is much more potential for social movement unionism in the new organization than there is when organizing drives are staff-driven, top-down affairs.

What about putting this approach to changing the movement into practice outside unions? Because other working-class organizations in Canada are few in number and mostly small, this means joining an existing group or starting from scratch. The situation is somewhat better in Quebec, where there is a *mouvement populaire* (popular movement) legacy of organizations of tenants, unemployed workers and city neighbourhood residents as well as university and CEGEP student unions that are more participatory than their equivalents on Canadian campuses (which have open membership meetings rarely or never).

Victoria's Communities Solidarity Coalition (CSC) was an outstanding example of a group based outside the workplace that hints at what part of a reinvented movement might look like.[30] In the wake of the 2001 election of an aggressively right-wing Liberal provincial government, several delegates to the Victoria Labour Council (some of whom were also involved in activism outside the unions) successfully proposed the launch of a coalition. The CSC brought together members and staff from HEU and other public sector unions, students, seniors' groups and others to fight the Campbell government's cuts and attacks on unions. "Regular folks" worked alongside radicals. Such close cooperation between union and community activists was an achievement, not least because of lingering suspicion from the 1983 betrayal of community groups by top union officials in B.C.'s Operation Solidarity debacle (Palmer 1987). At its peak, the CSC, whose inner core numbered between five and fifteen, had a flying squad of 250 people that could be mobilized for early-morning events and could draw a couple of thousand people to rallies. CSC activism was critical to the successful shut-down of Duncan in a trial Day of Defiance officially sponsored by the B.C. Federation of Labour. The CSC later used mass direct action to shut down government offices and the local university in Victoria's first Day of Defiance in October 2002, which it initiated. Another day of action in Victoria in May 2003 involved members of the Songhees First Nation and created new links between non-indigenous activists and indigenous people. The CSC also mobilized support for strikes by ferry workers and HEU. In October 2005, CSC activists came up with the plan used to shut down Victoria during a day of solidarity with striking teachers organized by B.C. Federation of Labour officials (Camfield 2009a). Activists who were involved in the CSC are now working to set up the Island Solidarity Centre as an "organizing space… where anyone can begin and sustain a campaign for justice, peace, women's rights, human rights" ("How?" 2009: 31).

Much of what workers' centres do is contributing in small ways to rein-venting the movement. As mentioned in Chapter Four, activists at Toronto's WAC do what they can to encourage non-unionized workers to organize themselves to fight to enforce their weak legal rights and to fight for stronger rights. They organize in languages other than English — a must when working among low-wage and precariously-employed wage-earners, many of whom are immigrant workers of colour — and strive to build unity and solidarity among workers. They have a vision of a dynamic workers' movement made up of both non-unionized workers and union members, and their efforts have helped to win small gains in legislation. Similarly, Montreal's IWC aims "to reach immigrant workers and provide a safe place for them where they can talk about and learn to act on work-related grievances" (Choudry et al. 2009: 107). Its activists' work includes doing education about workers' rights, organizing and the history of the working-class movement, offering a program that teaches both basic computer skills and workers' rights, campaigning on issues that affect immigrant workers and supporting union organizing among them (11–12). The kind of ongoing work done by WAC and IWC activists and staff is not as dramatic as the big actions that the CSC was able to organize at a time when many people in B.C. were prepared to protest and resist, but this does not make it less important. Developing people who work in non-union workplaces as organizers and linking them together can help to remake the movement. Some of this is also being done by a number of the small activist groups discussed in Chapter Four whose focus is not only or mainly on workplace rights, such as NOII groups, Justicia for Migrant Workers and militant anti-poverty organizations such as OCAP.

Publications and educational activity independent of the union officialdom also have an important role to play in strengthening efforts to change unions from below and build other workers' organizations. The single best example of this is *Labor Notes*. Originally founded in 1979 "to serve as a means of communication among insurgents in different unions" (Moody 1988: 246), this unique little U.S. monthly magazine and its website carry news and analysis for union and workers' rights activists and promote democratic, militant and solidaristic worker organizing. Its staff and supporters also organize a conference every two years where hundreds of like-minded people from different unions, activist groups, regions and countries (including Canada and Quebec) share ideas and experiences. They also put on smaller-scale workshops. In addition, *Labor Notes* publishes and distributes books for activists, including *The Troublemaker's Handbook* (Slaughter 2005), a guide to workplace activism. There is no equivalent of *Labor Notes* north of the border.[31] One reason for this is that it is very hard for people to obtain sizeable amounts of money for organizations that are independent of the union officialdom, especially if they are seen as critical of the officialdom. In the U.S., foundation funding for left-wing activist groups and projects is easier to obtain, although that creates its own problems (see Incite! 2007).

Of course, publishing and educational work can be done on a smaller scale than running a magazine. Discussion groups, book clubs, forums, workshops, day schools, websites, pamphlets — all can be useful for people working to change unions from below or build other movement organizations if they address issues that matter in an accessible way (without the jargon of academia or the radical left). All have the potential to help workers become more effective organizers and can be ways of generating and spreading new ideas as well as sharing lessons of past struggles such as these:

> Don't be intimidated by authority; never give up; if you are blocked
> in one way, find another avenue; think creatively and use the rights
> you have in new ways; treat the established channels with the con-
> tempt they deserve; rely upon your own strength. (Gray 2009)

These conclusions are drawn by Stan Gray from workplace health and safety
activism, but they are relevant to anyone who wants to help build a better
working-class movement from below.

Seeds of Hope

There is no hiding the fact that today the number of people in Canada and
Quebec involved in efforts to reform unions from below or in community-
based workers' organizations is small. One reason for this is that the shrink-
age of union density and the decay of unions as working-class movement
organizations has been slower and less dramatic than in the U.S. As a result,
the severity of the movement's problems is less obvious. Another is the difficulty of getting funding for initiatives that involve paid staff. The decline
of infrastructures of dissent and left-wing politics discussed in Chapter Six
have an important impact, too: few people are exposed to ideas about a different kind of workers' movement and even fewer have the opportunity to
learn from experienced radical activists how to organize effectively with a
perspective of promoting democracy, solidarity and militancy.

The good news is that even in difficult times there *are* people who, in the
words of a recently-retired CEP activist, "basically understand that there is a
class struggle and that we're getting our asses kicked."[32] Some of them are
people who are already organizing in a "from below" way. Others see the
need for change in order to fight back more effectively but are not consistently
taking this approach. Such workers are involved in doing things differently,
trying to make the kinds of changes that are needed in the movement.

Recent years have been tough for working-class movement activists, but
there are still moments when people are able to do things in ways that are
quite different from how they are usually done in the movement. Such seeds
of hope are very poorly reported and deserve to be better-known. What fol-
lows is just a sampling from the past decade, organized under the headings
of the different ways in which the movement needs to change (some could
be listed under more than one).

More Democracy

- CUPE 3903's victorious eleven-week strike of 2000–01 was organized
  in a highly democratic way. Membership control was exerted through
  frequent general meetings attended by hundreds of people. Many
  important decisions were made in these meetings, not by the executive

or bargaining team, both of which were accountable to members at mass meetings. Open strike committee meetings happened almost daily. Some decisions about picketing were made by picketers at each location.[33]

- Members of CAW Local 4209 in Winnipeg elect a very large executive. Instead of having the people elected to two particular positions automatically become full-time officers, the executive decides after the election which two persons are best suited to be the full-timers. This deters people from running for a position because they want to get away from the workplace rather than because they want to do the work that comes with serving in the position.[34]

- In 2005, a number of BCTF activists proposed to their union's AGM that in the event of a strike, the executive could not direct members to return to work before members had voted to end the strike. The motion passed. It helped the executive resist pressure from top B.C. Federation of Labour officials to agree to a poor deal and end the BCTF's October 2005 strike without a membership vote (as the HEU executive had done in 2004).[35]

More Activists

- In the summer of 2009, Winnipeg CUPW activists drew dozens of members of the local to a pair of participatory workshops. Billed as "activist strategy sessions," these were designed to draw more people into becoming active and to give them ideas about how to resist management on the shop floor. The workshops helped build the local's activist base.[36]

- The leaders of the Halifax-Dartmouth and District Labour Council have been rebuilding the council as an activist organization for solidarity with workplace and community-based struggles in the region. In 2009, council delegates (whose average age has fallen as more young unionists have become involved) unanimously adopted the slogan "Capitalism isn't working for workers."[37]

Better Activists

- CUPW activists have organized tours that take officers and rank-and-file members to Mexico for first-hand experience of the *maquiladora* factories of northern Mexico and to meet activists who organize in the region. "I take good-hearted trade unionists to Mexico and I bring back angry, determined, passionate warriors in defence of the labour movement. It rips off life-long blinders," said a tour organizer (in Bocking 2007: 23).

- The Popular Education and Action Project, formed in Toronto in early 2009, organized two day-schools that brought together activists, mostly in community-based groups, for radical education on the economic crisis and building resistance. One event was geared to preparing participants to do popular education themselves (Teller 2009).

- CUPW runs a Union Education Program of four one-week residential sessions. It is "NOT a tool course" but instead looks at issues including class, racism, sexism and heterosexism and at history in order to "develop our base of socially conscious, well-informed activists."[38]

Grassroots Leadership that Reflects the Working Class

- On campuses, in schools and on the streets in cities across Canada and Quebec, young people of colour are at the forefront of action for the rights of migrants, against racism and in support of the struggle of the people of Palestine against Israeli apartheid.[39] This activism has the potential to feed into the development of a new multiracial layer of grassroots leaders in unions and other organizations.

More Militancy

- In October 2005, thousands of B.C. union members (mostly in CUPE) took part in rotating regional sympathy strike action to support the province-wide teachers' strike. More than 20,000 CUPE school board workers respected BCTF picket lines throughout the strike. This action defied the law, as did the teachers' strike itself (Camfield 2009a).
- In July 2008, hundreds of non-unionized workers at Progressive Moulded Products in Vaughan, most of them immigrant workers of colour, responded to the employer's decision to lay off the entire workforce by blockading and then picketing the plant for more than two weeks (Ng 2009).
- Thousands of protestors at Vancouver airport prevented the deportation of disabled refugee claimant Laibar Singh in December 2007.[40]
- At the 2005 CLC convention, Carol Wall received the support of thirty-seven percent of votes cast in the contested election for CLC president, even though the heads of all the CLC's affiliates except CUPW urged delegates to vote for Ken Georgetti. Wall clearly called for mobilizing workers and criticized "the single-minded focus on back room lobbying" (Levant 2005: 5).

More Independence

- CAW members organized under the banner of CAW Members for Real Fairness challenged their official leadership's promotion of the 2007 "Framework for Fairness" deal with Magna within the union. In 2008, CAW members at Magna-owned Mississauga Seating rejected the attempt of the national leadership to get them to accept the deal, which would have taken away rights from their collective agreement, including the right to strike and their independent union representation in the workplace (Rosenfeld 2008a).
- Workers at Ford Oakville rejected the concessionary CAW-Ford master

agreement by a two-thirds majority — the first time workers at a major auto plant in Canada had voted down a deal recommended by their top officials (Gibb 2008; Gindin 2008).

Commitment to Mobilizing and Organizing the Entire Working Class
- The volunteers and staff of Toronto's WAC and Montreal's IWC actively seek to organize non-unionized workers, many of whom are precariously employed in occupations the union officialdom treats as too difficult or impossible to organize.
- Justicia for Migrant Workers activists based in Toronto and Vancouver continue to build relationships with people who come to Canada on temporary work visas to work in agriculture and to support these non-unionized workers, who suffer bad working and living conditions, isolation, intimidation and racism.[41]
- CUPW organizers are working to help bicycle and car couriers in Toronto to unionize, opening a storefront courier workers' centre and taking a long-term approach (Ryan 2009).

Deeper and Broader Solidarity
- Activists in CUPE 4308 in Toronto have made their local a consistent supporter of social justice struggles, including those led by OCAP and NOII (whose websites are linked from the local's homepage, along with that of *Labor Notes*).
- OCAP publicly supported the Toronto municipal workers' strike of 2009 (OCAP 2009). It did so despite the difficulties the strike caused for people on social assistance and the hostility to OCAP of the leaderships of both CUPE 79 and 416.
- HEU actively supported Victoria's CSC, assigning a staffer to work for the group.
- The large turnout at the May 2009 Stewards Assembly in Toronto showed the willingness of many local union activists to support each other's struggles.
- Unionists have provided "some of the best and most sustained support for Six Nations" indigenous people who reclaimed land near Caledonia, Ontario. This has included the work of rank-and-file members of different unions in the Caledonia group Community Friends and USW 1005 members from Stelco in Hamilton who mobilized to support the indigenous people's blockade, organized educationals in their local and donated money (Keefer 2007).
- Several union bodies have voted to deepen solidarity with the Palestinian people by joining the international campaign for Boycott, Divestment and Sanctions against Israel, despite heated attacks from pro-Israel groups. CUPE-Ontario was first, in 2006, followed by CUPW and the Fédération

nationale des enseignantes et des enseignants du Québec (Young 2009). CUPE-Ontario International Solidarity Committee members have carried out extensive educational activities for CUPE members.

- CUPE's Global Justice Committee supported a 2009 "Worker to Worker Solidarity Exchange" that toured Filipino unionists across Canada and Quebec and took CUPE members to the Philippines in 2010 with the goal of building an ongoing relationship with Filipino unions whose activists face violence, even assassination (Schwartz 2009a).

More Radicalism

- In 2004, workers at the Jonquiere Soderburg aluminum smelter in Arvida, Quebec, were told by their employer, Alcan, that the plant would be closed ten years sooner than had been agreed to by their union, a CAW affiliate. In response, workers occupied the plant and kept it running under workers' control (Niemeijer 2004).
- Members of NOII groups and other like-minded activists have contested the idea that only citizens and migrants who have permanent resident status really matter. They have opposed deportations. They have campaigned to defend wage-earners on work visas and non-status people's access to public services. They have linked these struggles with those of indigenous people. They have demanded reforms that would grant status to all residents, despite the "national security" fearmongering that many politicians and the corporate media have pushed since 9/11. Their approach challenges the divisions in the working class between people who have Canadian citizenship status and those who do not and between indigenous and non-indigenous people, divides that have usually been ignored by union activists in recent decades.
- An October 2009 gathering in Toronto brought together people from a number of community-based activist groups, unions and socialist groups who shared a commitment to building the working-class movement. Out of it the Greater Toronto Workers' Assembly was formed (Rosenfeld and Fanelli 2010).
- After hearing from speakers, including a representative of France's radical Solidaires union federation, delegates at the 2008 congress of the Fédération Interprofessionnelle de la Santé du Québec, the Quebec union of registered nurses, nursing assistants and cardio-respiratory care workers, voted in favour of adopting social movement unionism in place of social unionism.[42]

Taken together, such examples show there are people within the working-class movement who strive to aid their fellow workers to organize themselves in ways that are very democratic, militant and solidaristic. Such activists are willing to do what makes sense to them, even if it means defying the law, the entrenched customs of "responsible" unionism and parliamentary politics and the union officers and staff who defend these customs. Some see themselves as trying to change the movement; others do not, even if their actions really do challenge entrenched ways of acting and thinking.

Whatever the intentions of those involved, most of the examples surveyed involve people acting in ways that fit with the perspective of reforming unions from below and building other movement organizations. They confirm that this perspective is not a dream with no connection to reality. It is a strategy that draws out the implications of what fine activists have done in the past and are doing today. Increasing the number of such activists and strengthening their efforts is the best way to work towards reinventing the movement.

No one has a crystal ball with which to predict the future of the working-class movement. More important, at the present time, the forces of people inside and outside the unions who are trying to organize in ways that go beyond the limits of bureaucratic contract unionism and parliamentary politics are too weak for anyone to be able to say where a reinvented movement is starting to emerge (as a perceptive observer might have said of industrial unions at the close of the 1800s) or to say with any certainty how it is most likely to emerge. Nevertheless, the reflections of veteran activist intellectual John Clarke are food for thought. Clarke believes that within unions

> when the change comes it's going to very much come from the rank and file, which means it's going to come from people who are, at present, going to work and probably don't even attend union meetings… people at the moment who think it is all bullshit.

He recognizes that "there are, of course, important union militants who have been hammering away for years" whose "body of experience" will "be invaluable" in what is "likely to be an explosive change," but contends that most of today's layer of union activists "has become politically narrowed and to a degree politically compromised" by bureaucratic unionism.[43] Only future events will show if this prediction is accurate or not.

Towards New Politics

Efforts to reinvent the working-class movement cannot avoid politics. This does not mean only the question of what to do around federal, provincial and municipal elections. As a CAW document written when the union's top leadership was at its most left-wing argues:

> We generally think of politics as being about who gets elected and what they do — that is, about governments. But even though this is how it's normally expressed, the essence of politics is really about power and change: whose interests and values get attention

and results, and how people organize to affect that. So politics is really about society and not just government. No matter who gets elected, as long as power in society remains basically in the hands of a minority, our lives are shaped by that minority's control (power) over production, investment, finances, and communications. (CAW 2000)

There is no better example of the importance of that minority's power and how workers' movements cannot escape politics than the global economic crisis that some have dubbed the Great Recession.

Beginning in 2007, governments of the advanced capitalist countries carried out "the most massive intervention to stabilize capitalism in its history." Some $20 *trillion* had been poured into the financial system or spent on economic stimulus by late 2009 (McNally 2010). In Canada and Quebec, even workers whose employers have been more or less untouched by the crisis had their savings savaged by plunges in financial markets. Most wage-earners with deferred wages saved in pension plans now face having to pay higher pension contributions and/or the prospect of a lower pension when they retire. Private and public sector employers have responded to the crisis by imposing or demanding pay and benefit cuts and by laying off employees. Politicians are debating how deeply to cut government programs and state funding to hospitals, social service agencies, school boards, universities and colleges, in the name of the sacred neoliberal cause of reducing deficits.[44] A new era of austerity measures lies ahead.

What people in unions and other organizations say and do in response to all this is deeply political. This is true of officials who claim to be "non-political" and who have accepted without question the massive transfer of funds (most of which come from taxes paid by the working class) to ailing corporations and that workers must give concessions and agree to cuts to social programs. CLC President Ken Georgetti's appeal to the leaders gathered for the G-20 summit in Toronto in June 2010 "not to move too quickly to austerity measures" and "not to chop public services" (Georgetti 2010) was a contradictory political stance of accepting neoliberal austerity while wanting to limit it. The decision of the leaders of the TYRLC to present people who attended their Stewards Assembly with CAW economist Jim Stanford's view that "the crisis was not caused by workers, it was caused by the greedy, irresponsible unproductive speculation of the financial sector" (in Schwartz 2009b: 1) was equally political. These positions are no more and no less political than the view that the crisis is rooted in capitalism itself (not merely in financial speculation) and that workers should oppose every effort to make them pay for capitalism's crisis, instead demanding that banks and other failing firms be nationalized and converted to provide useful services and goods on a not-for-profit basis and that state debt should be repudiated.

Sometimes workplace and community struggles directly raise big political questions. For example, should public sector unionists accept government claims that services and jobs must be cut because deficits must be lowered? What is the best way to respond when workers who are Canadian citizens demand that their employer be made to hire unemployed Canadians instead of employing migrants who hold temporary work visas? Sooner or later, every activist trying to organize within a union or as part of another movement organization must also deal with political questions that transcend the immediate issues that come up in collective bargaining or campaigns directed at an employer, landlord, government official or any other single target. What is to be done about climate change? Should we support the Canadian military's participation in NATO's occupation of Afghanistan? How to respond to the demands of indigenous people and Quebec for national rights? How should working-class organizations relate to the existing political parties? In the long run, how should society change so that people can meet their needs and develop their capabilities, and what should be done to make that change happen?

In order to be able to respond to such questions in ways that help to make the working-class movement stronger and to change it, activists need different politics than those that are influential today in workers' organizations. A political outlook based on collective bargaining, lobbying and support for the NDP or for whichever political candidate is seen as the "least bad" is utterly inadequate. It gives people very little guidance in figuring out how to grapple with political issues like the ones mentioned above. It does not try to alter the inconsistent ways of thinking about politics that people learn at home, in school, in the workplace, in places of worship and from the media.[45] Even worse is the outlook that unions should "stay out of politics" and not concern themselves with anything beyond grievances and bargaining with employers, and that community-based groups should only advocate for the rights of those they claim to represent. Both viewpoints also implicitly endorse the way that society is currently structured, at most seeking whatever minor social reforms mainstream politicians are willing to support. Neither offers anything to a decaying working-class movement.

What is called for as an alternative is working-class politics. The CAW document from 2000 quoted above describes working-class politics in this way:

> Behind it, is the idea of developing the working class into a political force: one that is independent of business, oppositional to the status quo, confident enough to counter the dominant ideas in society with

an alternative common sense, and able to combine the defence of working people in their daily struggles with a longer term vision. Working class politics is, in short, about building a movement for social change.

Unionists who are trying to change unions from below and like-minded activists involved in community organizing are already working to build highly democratic organizations through which people can exercise more control over their lives. A democratic working-class politics aims to extend these essential small struggles into a long-term effort to create a genuinely democratic society, one that is no longer run by a small, wealthy and powerful minority.

Working-class politics is an entirely different way of doing politics than what is on offer from the NDP or the bulk of the union officialdom. The CAW leadership soon abandoned its flirtation with this perspective, which involves uniting workers to try to build a class-wide force for social change. This outlook offers people trying to change the working-class movement a framework for dealing with political issues that is consistent with their movement-building goals. Asking "How does this affect our efforts to develop the working class into a force for social change?" or "What should we say and do about this issue if that is our goal?" can help people to navigate treacherous political waters sown with mines laid by politicians, capitalists, top union officials and others who do not want to see a stronger, different workers' movement.

However, for an alternative politics to be truly useful for people who want to reinvent the movement, they cannot be politics that simply seek to mobilize and unite workers to change society. What is needed are politics that seek to combat all forms of oppression as part of developing the working class into a political force. Sexism, racism, heterosexism, the oppression of people with disabilities and the domination of some nations by others directly harm people who are oppressed. They also give at least some measure of privilege to people in dominant groups, including workers who are white, male and/or heterosexual. The division of the working class by oppression into unequal groups creates many obstacles to building a movement for social change. Simply calling on workers to unite without addressing these forms of oppression is a recipe for failure. Thus to be really effective, working-class politics need to fight against every form of inequality now and work towards the goal of liberation for all. One can call this anti-racist feminist working-class politics.[46]

A central political issue for supporters of working-class politics is what stance to take towards capitalism. This is not an abstract point. Business lobby groups, politicians, governments and capitalists themselves often argue that certain actions they undertake are important because they are good for business or "the economy" — in other words, capitalism. Unionized private sector workers come up against the corporate drive for profit and the fact that firms that do badly in the competitive war can go under. Public sector unionists confront the problem that their jobs and the services they deliver must be funded and the last thing that neoliberal governments want to do is raise taxes — especially taxes paid by corporations and the rich — even when deficits are rising. These are real constraints that exist because we live in a capitalist society. What attitude should workers have to these constraints? Should they buy into trying to make firms more profitable? Should they shoulder responsibility for reducing deficits? Should they try to make capitalism work better, as the NDP traditionally argued? Should they accept that TINA to capitalism?

Open discussion and debate of such questions is important for the working-class movement. There are different opinions about them among people who are working together to change their unions from below or build community-based movement organizations. Some people oppose concessions, layoffs, privatization, cutbacks, ecologically-destructive corporate practices and other outrages but do not draw the conclusion that capitalism itself is the root cause and must be rejected.[47] This position can be called anti-neoliberal but not anti-capitalist. It underpins, for example, John Cartwright's call for "the political power needed to overcome the natural instincts of global capitalism" and create a "green, prosperous future" (Cartwright 2009).

Others accept the analysis (which I share) that the attacks we face are caused by dynamics inherent to capitalism as a system. From this perspective, capitalism must always be a profit-driven system that causes great harm to humanity and other species. It is not like a beast whose instincts can be tamed, as Cartwright suggests. This makes capitalism fundamentally unethical, contrary to what is good. As the Great Recession and subsequent austerity measures have shown so clearly, even the gains of better-off workers in rich countries can be snatched away by this profit-driven socio-economic system. People who do not oppose capitalism risk agreeing that workers should at least sometimes help firms be profitable and accept responsibility for lowering state deficits. This amounts to identifying with the needs of capital, which are contrary to the needs of human beings (Lebowitz 2006). Doing this leads workers to make concessions, limit their own struggles and form alliances with their employer or state instead of with other workers. This turns workers' organizations away from defending workers' interests and towards becoming tools of capital. Anyone looking for evidence of where this can lead need only look again at unions in the U.S. (Moody 2007), Quebec (Bouchard 2009) and Canada today. The logical conclusion of this analysis is that working-class politics should be clearly anti-capitalist. Workers should reject responsibility for managing a system they do not control. Of course, activists should try to improve the conditions of people's lives now, which includes fighting for better laws and other measures within this capitalist society. But trying to win gains in the here and now through collective struggle is very different from the traditional social democratic strategy (abandoned by the NDP as its leaders accepted neoliberalism) of trying to manage capitalism in a way that helps workers — a futile and dangerous endeavour.

Whether capitalism itself should be rejected is an important question for debate. There are others, too. Is there a possible and desirable alternative to capitalism? If not, what does that mean? If so, what is it and how might it be created? What would the role of the working-class movement be in transforming society?[48] What is the connection between working to reinvent the working-class movement from below and struggling for an alternative to capitalism? What stance should workers take to the activities of the Canadian state and corporations abroad (see Gordon 2010)? What should unions do about climate change? Can market-based schemes like "cap and trade" reduce greenhouse gas emissions? Does the CLC's call for "a drastic and dramatic slowdown on any further expansion" (in Annis 2008) of the Alberta Tar Sands go far enough?

Another important political question is how to relate to the struggles of indigenous peoples. Canada is not just a capitalist society. It is a colonial-settler state, a state built on the conquest of indigenous peoples and, in a different way, on the conquest of Quebec (Adams 1989; Gordon 2010). Taking the slogan "an injury to one is an injury to all" seriously should lead worker activists to oppose colonialism and national oppression and support the right of indigenous peoples to determine their own future (and Quebec's right to self-determination, too). One of the implications of this is the need to be careful that workers' economic demands do not harm indigenous people and their lands (Gordon 2009). People who practice business unionism, with their embrace of corporate objectives, have generally been simply hostile to the demands and aspirations of indigenous people. Part of the union officialdom "align[s] itself with government-funded indigenous organizations" like those of the Assembly of First Nations "that also want economic development," such as the construction associated with the 2010 Winter Olympics in B.C. and the Alberta Tar Sands. Unionists have allied with "decolonization [oriented] grassroots indigenous resistance"[49] only rarely. But why would working-class activists want to partner with corporate-oriented indigenous leaders, the counterparts of the pro-capitalist labour officialdom, rather than more militant and radical indigenous activists?[50]

People who are busy dealing with grievances, campaigning against privatization or mobilizing to prevent a deportation or pressure an employer to pay unpaid wages may feel they do not have time to worry about politics. There is a real need to deal with these and other matters that are urgent because they affect people's well-being right now. But it is a mistake to focus only on specific immediate struggles and neglect bigger questions. Not arguing for anti-racist feminist working-class politics in the movement leaves it under the direction of supporters of some version of neoliberalism or of traditional social democracy, with its confidence in making change through the ballot box. When supporters of working-class politics do not continue to educate themselves, they fail to prepare for the arguments that will always happen whenever they try to convince others to oppose what employers, governments or union officials say people must accept. The question is not if to deal with politics, but how.

Unfortunately, at present, there is no significant and attractive organization committed to working-class politics in Canada, only tiny radical left political groups.[51] In Quebec, these are not the politics of most of the leaders or members of Québec Solidaire, but some supporters of such politics belong to Quebec's left-wing party. At this stage, the best that people who want to build support for this kind of politics within unions and other organizations can do is to conduct educational activities such as discussion groups, forums and workshops, whether organized officially (through a union local's education committee, for example) or independently. Such education is important, since among most people at the forefront of today's struggles "what is missing is not outrage, not militancy, but a more analytical and strategic awareness of the class issues and implications raised in struggle, whether everyday or explosive" (Cohen 2006: 177). Education that develops people's ability to analyze and think strategically can contribute to building a new infrastructure of dissent that nurtures workers' capacity for collective action.

Future struggles will probably lead to many more people becoming open to the approach to changing the workers' movement argued for in these pages. One factor that will affect how much change from below will happen when new opportunities arise is how many people with this vision have already made a serious commitment to digging in for the long haul as rank-and-file activists in unions, workers' centres and other organizations.[52] Inspiring protests and resistance will also make more people interested in radical ideas, as happened in Canada and Quebec at the height of the global justice movement between 2000 and 2002.[53] This will create new openings for all who agree with Oscar Olivera, a leading figure of social movement unionism in Bolivia: "They can privatize everything, but not our dreams. While we are still alive we will always fight for our dreams" (Olivera 2009).

Notes

1. As of late 2010, Change to Win had shrunk to four unions and UNITE HERE had returned to the AFL-CIO (minus the parts of the union that followed former top

UNITE officials in breaking away to form Workers United, affiliated with SEIU).

2. For example, see the chapters in part II of Kumar and Schenk 2006.
3. Here I am quoting from comments by Brian McDougall on a draft of this book.
4. <labouraction.ca>. The other two elements were "the leadership and resources necessary to build and sustain long-term campaigns" and "the ability to combine formal electoral political organizing with the building of popular movements."
5. See <labouraction.ca>.
6. The unionism practiced by top UNITE HERE officials is not identical to that of SEIU's top leaders. However, there is much more similarity than UNITE HERE's leaders would admit, as four activists with experience in UNITE HERE have argued (Abbott-Klafter et al. 2009).
7. Uncritical endorsement of the ideas and actions of the TYRLC leadership and of the approach laid out in Fletcher and Gapasin 2008 is evidence of support for mobilization unionism. The TYRLC organized a day-long event with Fletcher on October 3, 2008.
8. For example, see the council's strategic directions documents at <labourcouncil.org>.
9. I am indebted to Sheila Wilmot for sharing her analysis of the TYRLC, which she is examining in her doctoral dissertation.
10. See <labourcouncil.ca> and <laboureducation.org>.
11. Abbott-Klafter et al. 2009 provides a valuable insiders' account of activism without democracy in UNITE HERE. A former organizer for a SEIU local in Ontario discusses her experiences of activism without democracy and reflects on its lessons for people considering taking union staff jobs in G 2007.
12. This describes itself as "an alliance of community, labour, social justice, youth and environmental organizations in the Toronto region... formed in 2008 to start a focused dialogue on how to improve living and working conditions in Canada's largest urban centre" <goodjobsforall.ca/?page_id=2>.
13. Each is entitled to two delegates who can vote except on TYRLC bylaws and in elections (e-mail from John Cartwright, September 17, 2009).
14. In fact, its leadership has been hostile to many radical community and union activists. John Clarke contrasts the "fairly good working relationship" between OCAP and the council in the early 1990s with Cartwright's "open hostility" (interview, June 10, 2009). Having a few radicals as elected officers, staffers and guest speakers has not caused the actions of the TYRLC to take a radical direction. It is worth remembering the reply of CIO leader John L. Lewis when queried about the number of radicals hired to work for the Steel Workers Organizing Committee (forerunner of the USW) during the 1930s: "Who gets the bird, the hunter or the dog?" <coalmininglabormuseum.com/main.html>
15. This was evident during the 2009 municipal workers' strike. See Chapter One, note 26.
16. For analysis of the global economic slump as a crisis of contemporary capitalism, see McNally 2009 and 2010.
17. See Downs 2009b for some reflections on this in a U.S. context.
18. Interview with John Humphrey, June 4, 2009.
19. Interview with NOII supporter, February 14, 2009.
20. For example, according to an untitled unpublished 2008 document by CUPE activist Katherine Nastovski, one of the impacts of CUPE-Ontario's Palestine solidarity efforts has been "seeing community activists finding an interest in being involved or

identifying with their union, which they otherwise would not be."

21. Interview with Euan Gibb, June 10, 2009.

22. Interview with Herman Rosenfeld, June 7, 2009.

23. This goal is unattainable for the working-class movement as a whole in a capitalist society, but the development of workers' capacities is certainly possible.

24. "A staff job in a local run by reform-minded officers, particularly those with a relationship to union reform movements, is likely to provide the best opportunity for promoting rank-and-file unionism from a union staff position" (Gonzalez, Phillips, et al. 2001: 22).

25. See the discussions of leadership in Parker and Gruelle 1999: 42–56; Slaughter 2005: 322–28; and Lynd and Lynd 2000.

26. Slaughter 2005 is a unique resource. On what may appear to be apathy, see Slaughter 2005: 7.

27. These observations stem from my personal experience as a member of CUPE 3903 at the time.

28. The Solidarity Caucus no longer exists.

29. On these flying squads, see Kuhling and Levant 2006. In the CAW, some members "were really developing strong horizontal linkages with each other… quite separate from the traditional structures of the union" through flying squads and other independent initiatives (interview with Euan Gibb, June 10, 2009).

30. This account draws on an interview with former CSC activists, February 16, 2009, and e-mails from former CSC activists, December 7 and 9, 2009.

31. A loose Quebec grouping influenced to some extent by it, Forum intersyndical, existed from 1998 to 2003 (see <mobilisation.org/rubrique24.html?lang=fr>).

32. Interview with Gene McGuckin, February 17, 2009.

33. But this democracy was only one of the reasons why the strike ended in victory. Favourable circumstances and strike issues that kept most members united behind the strike also contributed to success in 2000–01. This was not understood by a later cohort of activists during CUPE 3903's even longer strike of 2008–09 (see Lafrance 2010 for an account and some critical assessment of this strike). McCreary 2009 makes some important points about the two strikes (though I disagree with his suggestion that the failings of some 3903 activists during the second strike were responsible for the fact that no solidarity strike action to support 3903 took place). CUPE 3903 is unusual because of the number of leftists in its membership (many left-wing students in Canada and Quebec and beyond are attracted to graduate studies at York University). For this reason, one should be careful not to generalize too much from the experiences of this local. But this, and its recent debacles, do not mean this local's past achievements can be dismissed.

34. Interview with Karen Naylor, January 9, 2009.

35. E-mail from BCTF activist Lisa Descary, December 14, 2009.

36. E-mail from CUPW activist Marc Roy, November 29, 2009.

37. Information from various communications with activists in Halifax.

38. <cupw.ca/1/2/0/0/4/index1.shtml?>.

39. On Israeli apartheid, see White 2009.

40. <mostlywater.org/laibar_singh_wins_another_temporary_stay>.

41. On migrant agricultural workers, see Basok 2002.

42. I was present at the congress. Whether the vote has actually led to much change in FIQ is questionable, but the explicit discussion of social movement unionism as an alternative to social unionism was extremely unusual.

43. Interview with John Clarke, June 10, 2009.
44. For a brief analysis of the political economy of deficit-reduction, see Camfield and Serge 2010.
45. For an interesting analysis of how working-class consciousness is shaped in contemporary society, see Seccombe and Livingstone 2000.
46. See McNally 2006: ch. 7 and Wilmot 2005.
47. This is the ideology of, for example, the Council of Canadians, most people on the left wing of the NDP, the majority of Québec Solidaire and prominent left figures like Maude Barlow, Naomi Klein, Linda McQuaig and Jim Stanford. For critiques, see Burgess 2009; Davidson 2009; McNally 2006: 83–131.
48. Of the many viewpoints in discussions among anti-capitalists today, Albert n.d., Lebowitz 2006, McNally 2006 and Milstein 2010 represent some of the most important. My own views are closest to McNally's. Of the many websites that publish a range of anti-capitalist perspectives in English, <znet.org> (run by Albert and some of his co-thinkers) is the single most important.
49. Interview with NOII supporter, February 14, 2009.
50. For an interesting attempt by a radical indigenous writer to summarize "the most basic changes… required to create a just relationship" between non-indigenous and indigenous people, see Alfred 2005: 268.
51. The Greater Toronto Workers' Assembly is an attempt to change this situation in one city. Most of the radical left political groups (a few of which pretend to be parties despite their tiny size) suffer from sectarianism: their members put their group's interests (such as recruiting more members or preserving themselves as separate groups) ahead of the interests of the working-class movement as a whole. Most also suffer from self-importance, dogmatic thinking and little or no internal democracy. The New Socialist Group and Socialist Project suffer least from these vices.
52. Despite their U.S. focus, the publications and conferences of *Labor Notes* are valuable for people in Canada and Quebec who share this commitment. Canadian and Quebec equivalents are sorely needed. See also the U.S. website <radicalsatwork. org>.
53. In Canada, the radicalization around global justice led to two attempts to build new left-wing political formations, the New Politics Initiative (see Rao 2004) and a few local efforts after the "Rebuilding the Left" conference held in Toronto in October 2000. Much of the youth radicalization went into a diffuse anarchism.

Suggested Further Readings and Resources

People looking to deepen their understanding of the contemporary work-ers' movement in Canada and Quebec have much less to choose from than people interested in the movement in the U.S. (because what happens in the U.S. has an important impact north of the border, Kim Moody's *US Labor in Trouble and Transition* and Steve Early's *The Civil Wars in US Labor* are well worth reading). Readers will find many books and articles listed in the references section of this book, but some sources deserve special mention.

Our Times bills itself as "Canada's independent labour magazine;" it publishes some interesting material, but not critical analysis of developments in the movement. There is no Canadian periodical that consistently covers events and issues in the way the monthly *Labor Notes* and its website <labornotes. org> do for the U.S. (they do publish some articles about what happens north of the border). A number of Canadian and Quebecois publications sometimes run useful articles related to the workers' movement: *The Bullet* and *Relay* <socialistproject.ca>, *New Socialist Webzine* <newsocialist.org>, *Canadian Dimension* <canadiandimension.ca>, *Briarpatch* <briarpatchmagazine.com>, *Presse Toi à Gauche* <pressegauche.org> and *À Bâbord!* <ababord.org>.

Thom Workman's *If You're in My Way, I'm Walking: The Assault on Working People Since 1970* is a good introduction to the neoliberal offensive against workers. Leo Panitch and Donald Swartz's *From Consent to Coercion: The Assault on Trade Union Freedoms* (third edition) looks in detail at attacks on union rights since the mid-1970s.

James Rinehart's *The Tyranny of Work: Alienation and the Labour Process* (fifth edition) is the best introduction to the organization of work in Canada. After that, try *Interrogating the New Economy: Restructuring Work in the 21st Century*, edited by Norene Pupo and Mark Thomas.

The history of the working-class movement is important for a number of reasons, including what it reveals about how the movement came to be in its present state and how workers' past victories were won. On the movement in Canada and Quebec, there is Craig Heron's *The Canadian Labour Movement: A Short History* (second edition) and Bryan Palmer's *Working-Class Experience:*

Rethinking the History of Canadian Labour (second edition). Paul Mason's *Live Working or Die Fighting: How the Working Class Went Global* is a good, lively introduction to the history of the movement internationally. The academic journal *Labour/Le Travail* publishes mainly historical articles on workers and their organizations, but also some pieces on recent developments. Sadly, very few worker activists in Canada ever write about their experiences. One exception is Stan Gray, who was named "The Greatest Canadian Shit Disturber" by *Canadian Dimension* <canadiandimension.com/articles/1953>.

Union activists and anyone interested in becoming one will find the *Labor Notes* book *A Troublemaker's Handbook 2* (2005) a must-have. *Democracy is Power* (1999), also from *Labor Notes*, is useful, too.

Any student thinking about working for a union should read Steve Early's essay "Then and Now — Thoughts on the 'Worker-Student Alliance'" <labornotes.org/node/1123>.

Anyone doing labour education will want *Education for Changing Unions* (2002), coauthored by five labour and community educators.

Concepts

This defines some terms that will be unfamiliar to many readers or whose specific meaning as used in this book is worth clarifying.

alienation: A "condition of objective powerlessness," "in which individuals have little or no control over" their work (Rinehart 2006: 14).

bureaucracy: A way of organizing society in which people are subject to formal rules that limit their ability to determine what they do and how they do it, rules they cannot easily change.

business unionism: An approach to union activity and ideology whose key features are a narrow focus on collective bargaining for wages and benefits, a generally cooperative approach to employers and a low level of democracy.

capitalism: A way of organizing society in which most goods and services are produced for sale as commodities by competing enterprises (privately or state-owned) and in which people's ability to work is a commodity.

contract unionism: Union activity and ideology whose central focus is the bureaucratic negotiation and administration of legally-binding collective agreements.

corporate unionism: An approach to union activity and ideology whose key features are its commitments to increasing the number of workers covered by collective agreements, partnerships with employers and highly centralized unions with a low level of democracy.

direct action: Collective action that attempts to disrupt the functioning of an organization or institution (examples include strikes, occupations and blockades).

dominant class (also ruling class): The employing class along with the government and the top ranks of the civil service, military and police.

employing class: The social class made up of persons who employ people who work for wages.

exploitation: The extraction of surplus labour from those who produce goods and services.

mobilization unionism: An approach to union activity and ideology that takes a militant stance towards employers, commits unions to working for social change against neoliberalism alongside community groups, treats extra-parliamentary political action as important and tries to increase membership participation, but which is not highly democratic.

neoliberalism: A form of capitalism that emerged after the end of the long period of economic expansion that followed the Second World War, at whose core is the weakening of barriers to corporate profit-making. The term is also used to refer to the ideology associated with this particular form of capitalism.

officer: A member who holds an elected or appointed position in a union.

official: A union officer or staff person.

officialdom: The social layer made up of union officers and staff.

people (or workers) of colour: People (or workers) who experience racism in society (the term racialized people is sometimes used today to mean the same thing). Note that indigenous people also experience racism, but in Canada, the term "people of colour" does not include indigenous people.

rank-and-file: Members who do not hold any official union position.

social unionism: An approach to union activity and ideology that is concerned with social and political issues not directly connected to the workplace as well as with collective bargaining.

social movement unionism: An approach to union activity and ideology that is highly democratic, takes a militant stance towards employers, commits unions to working against neoliberalism for social change alongside community groups and treats extra-parliamentary political action as important.

staffer: A person who works for a union.

substitutionism: A person or group of persons acting in ways that do not assist others to act for themselves.

union wage premium: The amount by which the pay of unionized workers is greater than the pay of non-unionized workers.

worker: Any member of the working class (whether working for wages or not).

working class: The social class made up of everyone who sells their ability to work to an employer in exchange for a wage (whether paid on an hourly basis or as a salary) and who does not wield truly substantial management authority, along with unemployed wage-earners and the unwaged people who live in households that depend on wage income.

References

Abbott-Klafter, Sean, et al. 2009. "Open Letter to All Those Concerned About the Labour Movement." *MRZine* <monthlyreview.org/mrzine/labor141009.html>.

Adams, Howard. 1989. *Prison of Grass: Canada from a Native Point of View*. Saskatoon: Fifth House.

Akyeampong, Ernest B. 2000. "Non-Unionized but Covered by Collective Agreement." *Perspectives on Labour and Income* 12 (Autumn): 33–38.

Albert, Michael. n.d. [2002]. *Parecon: Life after Capitalism* <zcommunications.org/zparecon/pareconlac.htm>.

Albo, Greg, and Dan Crow. 2005. "New Bargaining Strategies? USWA and the New Economy." *MRZine* <mrzine.monthlyreview.org/albocrow190905.html>.

Albo, Greg, and Herman Rosenfeld. 2009. "Toronto City Workers on Strike: Battling Neoliberal Urbanism." *The Bullet* 232 (July 2) <socialistproject.ca/bullet/bullet232.html>.

Alfred, Taiaiake. 2005. *Wasáse: Indigenous Pathways of Action and Freedom*. Peterborough, ON: Broadview.

Allen, Bruce. 2009a. "The Crisis in Auto." *New Socialist* 66: 13–16.

_____. 2009b. "The Strike of 1978–79 Remembered." *Sudbury Star* n.d. <thesudburystar.com/ArticleDisplay.aspx?e=1702304>.

_____. 2006. "Inside the CAW Jacket." *New Socialist* 57 (July–August): 18–20.

Annis, Roger. 2009. "Unite Union Wins Gains for Vulnerable Workers in New Zealand." *The Bullet* 216 (May 13) <socialistproject.ca/bullet/bullet216.html>.

_____. 2008. "Canadian Labour Congress Discusses Climate Change." *Climate and Capitalism* May 29. <climateandcapitalism.com/?p=446>.

Anonymous. 2009. "The Toronto Labour Council's Stewards's Assembly." *New Socialist Webzine* <newsocialist.org/index.php?option=com_content&view=article&id=99%3Athe-toronto-labour-councils-stewards-assembly&Itemid=102>.

Austin, Cathy, Lisa Descary and Katherine Nostovski. 2007. "She Went On to Organize: Interviews with Women Labour Activists." Interview by Sandra Sarner. *New Socialist* 60 (Spring): 11–14.

Baron, Alain. 2009. "Unionism of Resistance: SUD-Solidaires and Radical Labor Action in France." *International Socialist Review* 66 (July–August): 13–14.

Barnett, Julia, and Carlo Fanelli. 2009. "Lessons Learned: Assessing the 2009 City of Toronto Strike and Its Aftermath." *New Socialist* 66: 26–29.

Basok, Tanya. 2002. *Tortillas and Tomatoes: Transmigrant Mexican Harvesters in Canada*. Montreal: McGill-Queen's University Press.

Bentham, Karen. 2007. "Labour's Collective Bargaining Record on Women's and Family Issues." In Gerald Hunt and David Rayside (eds.), *Equity, Diversity, and Canadian Labour*. Toronto: U of Toronto Press.

Bickerton, Geoff. 2007. "First FFA Collective Agreement Restricts Workers Democratic Rights." *The Bullet* 75 (November 26) <socialistproject.ca/bullet/075.html>.

_____. 2006. "Labour Stands Up Against War." *Canadian Dimension* (July-August) <canadiandimension.com/articles/1848/>.

Bickerton, Geoff, and Catherine Stearns. 2006. "The Workers' Organizing and Resource

References

Centre in Winnipeg." In Pradeep Kumar and Christopher Schenk (eds.), *Paths to Union Renewal: Canadian Experiences*. Peterborough, ON: Broadview.

Bickerton, Geoff, and Rosemary Warskett. 2005. "Contractors or Disguised Employees? A Case Study of Couriers in Winnipeg." *Just Labour* 6/7: 23–30.

Bocking, Paul. 2007. "Union Sunrise: Canadian-Mexican Labour Solidarity." *Our Times* August-September: 19–24.

Bouchard, Sebastien. 2009. "Réflexions sur le Mouvement Syndical et la Crise." *Nouveaux Cahiers du Socialisme* 2: 185–96.

Brennan, Barry. 2005. "Canadian Labor Today: Partial Successes, Real Challenges." *Monthly Review* 57.2 (June) <monthlyreview.org/0605brennan.htm>.

Briskin, Linda. 2009. "Cross-Constituency Organizing: A Vehicle for Union Renewal." In Janice R. Foley and Patricia L. Baker (eds.), *Unions, Equity, and the Path to Renewal*. Vancouver: University of British Columbia Press.

Buott, Kyle. 2009. "How Canadians Won Single Payer." *Labor Notes* 366 (September): 7.

Burgess, Bill. 2009. "Improve Capitalism or Replace It?" *Socialist Voice* February 17 <socialistvoice.ca/?p=367>.

Burgmann, Verity. 1998. *Green Bans, Red Union: Environmental Activism and the New South Wales Builders Labourers' Federation*. Sydney: University of New South Wales Press.

Byers, Jim. 2007. "Miller Leaves NDP, Shifts to Neutral." *Toronto Star* April 18: B1.

Camfield, David. 2009a. "Sympathy for the Teacher: Labour Law and Transgressive Workers' Collective Action in British Columbia, 2005." *Capital and Class* 99: 81–107.

_____. 2009b. "What Is Trade Union Bureaucracy? Theoretical Considerations and the Canadian Case." Paper presented to the Annual Meetings of the Society for Socialist Studies, Ottawa.

_____. 2008. "The Working-Class Movement in Canada: An Overview." In Miriam Smith (ed.), *Group Politics and Social Movements in Canada*. Peterborough, ON: Broadview

_____. 2007a. "CUPE's Sympathy Strikes in British Columbia, October 2005: Raising the Bar for Solidarity." *Just Labour* 11: 35–42.

_____. 2007b. "Renewal in Canadian Public Sector Unions: Neoliberalism and Union Praxis." *Relations industrielles/Industrial Relations* 62,2: 282–304.

_____. 2006. "Neoliberalism and Working Class Resistance in British Columbia: The Hospital Employees' Union Struggle, 2002–2004." *Labour/Le Travail* 57 (Spring): 9–41.

_____. 2005. "Public Sector Reform and the Future of Public Sector Unions." *Review of Economic and Social Trends in Manitoba* (Canadian Centre for Policy Alternatives —Manitoba) 5,1: 1–4.

_____. 2004/2005. "Reorienting Class Analysis: Working Classes as Historical Formations." *Science and Society* 68, 4: 421–46.

_____. 2002. "Class, Politics and Social Change: The Remaking of the Working Class in 1940s Canada." Doctoral dissertation, York University.

_____. 2000. "Assessing Resistance in Harris's Ontario, 1995–1999." In Mike Burke, Colin Mooers and John Shields (eds.), *Restructuring and Resistance: Canadian Public Policy in an Age of Global Capitalism*. Halifax: Fernwood Publishing.

Camfield, David, and Daniel Serge. 2010. "The Deficit: THEIR Problem, Not Ours." *New Socialist Webzine*. April 26. <newsocialist.org/index.php?option=com_content&view=article&id=168:the-deficit-their-problem-not-ours-&catid=51:analysis&Itemid=98>

Campbell, Bruce. 2009. "The Global Economic Crisis and Its Canadian Dimension: Economic Downturn Is Already as Bad as in the Early 1930s." <policyalternatives.ca>

Carroll, William K., and R.S. Ratner (eds.). 2005. *Challenges and Perils: Social Democracy in Neoliberal Times*. Black Point and Winnipeg: Fernwood Publishing.

Cartwright, John. 2009. "Green Jobs and Power." *Our Times* 28, 5 (October-November): 40.

CAW (Canadian Auto Workers). 2009. *Building the Union in Hard Times*. <caw.ca/en/7753. htm>

_____. 2000. *Working-Class Politics in the 21ˢᵗ Century*. <caw.ca/crisis1/index.asp>

CBCNews.ca. 2009a. "Windsor, Ont., Civic Strike Ends." At <cbc.ca/canada/toronto/ story/2009/07/24/windsor-strike-vote072409.html>

_____. 2009b. "Final Settlements Reached in Lawsuit Against Crocus Investment Fund." At <cbc.ca/canada/manitoba/story/2009/04/22/mb-crocus-settlement.html>

Cheung, Leslie. 2006. *Racial Status and Employment Outcomes*. [Ottawa:] Canadian Labour Congress.

Choudry, Aziz, et al. 2009. *Fight Back: Workplace Justice for Immigrants*. Halifax and Winnipeg: Fernwood Publishing.

CLC (Canadian Labour Congress). 2009. *Statement to the Standing Committee on Finance Hearing on Bill C-10 Regarding the EI Provisions of the 2009 Budget*. <canadianlabour.ca>

_____. 1998. *Report of the CLC Women's Symposium: Bargaining for Equality and No Easy Recipes: Feminist Organizing Models*. Ottawa: Canadian Labour Congress.

Coburn, David. 2009. "Inequality and Health." In Leo Panitch and Colin Leys (eds.), *Socialist Register 2010*. London, New York and Halifax: Merlin, Monthly Review and Fernwood.

_____. 2004. "Beyond the Income Inequality Hypothesis: Class, Neo-Liberalism, and Health Inequalities." *Social Science and Medicine* 58: 41–56.

Cohen, Sheila. 2006. *Ramparts of Resistance: Why Workers Lost Their Power and How to Get it Back*. London and Ann Arbor: Pluto.

Conway, John. 2009. "Wall Declares War on Organized Labour in Saskatchewan." *The Bullet* 239 (July 13) <socialistproject.ca/bullet/239.php>

Cooke, Murray. 2007. "Structural Changes and Political Challenges: The New Democratic Party in the 1990s." Paper presented at the Annual Meetings of the Canadian Political Science Association. <cpsa-acsp.ca/papers-2007/Cooke.pdf>

Cranford, Cynthia J., et al. 2006. "Community Unionism and Labour Movement Renewal: Organizing for Fair Employment." In Pradeep Kumar and Christopher Schenk (eds.), *Paths to Union Renewal: Canadian Experiences*. Peterborough: Broadview.

Crinson, Iain, and Chris Yuill. 2008. "What Can Alienation Theory Contribute to an Understanding of Social Inequalities of Health?" *International Journal of Health Services* 38, 3: 455–70.

Cumming, Douglas. 2009. "Labour-Sponsored Funds Didn't Work." *Financial Post* February 10. <financialpost.com/executive/story.html?id=1271483>

CUPE Joint Bargaining News. 2009. "Recession Is No Excuse for Gutting Contract Language." [CUPE Locals 79 and 416] 3 (April 14): 1.

Davidson, Neil. 2009. "Shock and Awe." *International Socialism* 124 (second series) <isj. org.uk/index.php4?id=587&issue=124#Davidson_44>

Davis, Mike. 1986. *Prisoners of the American Dream: Politics and Economy in the History of the US Working Class*. London and New York: Verso.

Dembinski, Ann, and Mark Ferguson. 2009. "Stronger Together: On Strike." *CUPE Joint Strike Bulletin* [CUPE Locals 79 and 416] 1 (26 June): 1.

Downs, Steve. 2009a. "Crisis of Capitalism, Challenge to the Movements." Video of a talk at the conference "Their Crisis/Our Movements — What's Next?" New York, November 13. <nysolidarity.org/09conference videos>

References

_____. 2009b. "Book Review: *Solidarity Divided*." <labornotes.org/node/2509>

_____. 2006. *Hell on Wheels: The Success and Failure of Reform in Transport Workers Union Local 100*. Detroit: Solidarity.

Early, Steve. 2011. *The Civil Wars in US Labor: Birth of a New Workers' Movement or Death Throes of the Old?* Chicago: Haymarket.

_____. 2009. *Embedded With Organized Labor: Journalistic Reflections on the Class War at Home.* New York: Monthly Review.

_____. 2008. "The Crisis in Organized Labor — As Viewed from the Inside and Out." *Znet.* <zmag.org/znet/viewArticle/17906>

Edelson, Miriam. 2009. "Confronting Racism in the Canadian Labour Movement: An Intergenerational Assessment." In Janice R. Foley and Patricia L. Baker (eds.), *Unions, Equity, and the Path to Renewal.* Vancouver: University of British Columbia Press.

Engler, Yves. 2008. "Quebec and Haiti." *Znet.* <zmag.org/znet/viewArticle/17145>

Engler, Yves, and Anthony Fenton. 2005. *Canada in Haiti: Waging War on the Poor Majority.* Vancouver and Black Point: RED and Fernwood Publishing.

Fine, Bob. 1984. *Democracy and the Rule of Law: Liberal Ideals and Marxist Critiques.* London and Sydney: Pluto.

FIQ. 2008. *Uniting Our Forces to Renew Our Action Together.* Montreal: Fédération interprofessionelle de la sante du Québec.

Fletcher, Bill Jr., and Fernando Gapasin. 2008. *Solidarity Divided: The Crisis in Organized Labor and a New Path Towards Social Justice.* Berkeley: University of California Press.

Foley, Janice R., and Patricia L. Baker. 2009. *Unions, Equity, and the Path to Renewal.* Vancouver: University of British Columbia Press.

Forrest, Anne. 1989. "The Rise and Fall of National Bargaining in the Canadian Meat-Packing Industry." *Relations industrielles/Industrial Relations* 44, 2: 393–406.

Frappier, André. 2009a. "FTQ et Fonds de Solidarité: L'Heure des Bilans." *À Bâbord!* 31 (October–November). <www.ababord.org/spip.php?article949>

_____. 2009b. "Lettre Ouverte aux Syndicalistes de la FTQ: Syndicalisme ou Rendement Financier, la FTQ à la Croisée des Chemins." *Presse Toi A Gauche* June 25. <pressegauche.org>

Fraser, Wayne, et al. 2007. "The Magna Sell-Out." *Financial Post* November 23. <financialpost.com/story.html?id=e9163705-0d0b-4664-bdcb-0d4c7ea5f5c8>

Freeman, Bill. 1982. *1005: Political Life in a Union Local.* Toronto: James Lorimer.

Fudge, Derek. 2006. *Collective Bargaining in Canada: Human Right or Canadian Illusion.* Second edition. Black Point and Winnipeg: Fernwood Publishing.

Fudge, Judy. 2008. "The Supreme Court of Canada and the Right to Bargain Collectively in Canada and Beyond." *Industrial Law Journal* 37, 1: 25–48.

Fudge, Judy, and Eric Tucker. 2001. *Labour Before the Law: The Regulation of Workers' Collective Action in Canada, 1900–1948.* Don Mills: Oxford University Press.

G., Katherine. 2007. Interview by Jeff R. Webber. "The Contradictions Facing Young Radicals in Union Staff Jobs." *New Socialist* 60 (Spring): 16–18.

Galabuzi, Grace-Edward. 2006. *Canada's Economic Apartheid: The Social Exclusion of Racialized Groups in the New Century.* Toronto: Canadian Scholar's.

Gapasin, Fernando. 2009. "Starting from the Beginning." *Znet.* <zmag.org/znet/viewArticle/22064>

Georgetti, Ken. 2010. "Statement by Ken Georgetti, President of the Canadian Labour Congress on Vandalism Surrounding Toronto G20 Meeting." June 26. <canadianlabour.ca/national/news/statement-ken-georgetti-president-canadian-labour-congress-vandalism-surrounding-toron>

Gibb, Euan. 2008. "The Oakville Update." *Workers for Union Renewal* 1 (October): 2–4 [Newsletter].

Gindin, Sam. 2009a. "The Auto Crisis: Placing Our Own Alternatives on the Table." *The Bullet* 200 (April 9). <socialistproject.ca/bullet/bullet200.html>

_____. 2009b. "Challenges for Public Sector Unions: Thinking Big to Win." *The Bullet* 264 (October 21). <socialistproject.ca/bullet/264.php>

_____. 2008. "The CAW and Panic Bargaining: Early Opening at the Big Three." *The Bullet* 105 (May 6). <socialistproject.ca/bullet/bullet105.html>

_____. 2007. "The CAW and Magna: Disorganizing the Working Class." *The Bullet* 65 (October 19). <socialistproject.ca/bullet/bullet065.html>

_____. 1998a. "Socialism with 'Sober Senses': Developing Workers' Capacities." In Leo Panitch and Colin Leys (eds.), *Socialist Register 1998*. Rendlesham, New York and Halifax: Merlin, Monthly Review and Fernwood.

_____. 1998b. "The Party's Over." *This Magazine* Nov-Dec: 13-15.

Globe and Mail. 2005. "Mayor's Team Waiting in Wings for Election Campaign to Begin." October 17: A10.

Globe Investor. 2009. "Chapter 5: Are LSIFs a Good Choice for Me?" <theglobeandmail. com/globe-investor/investment-ideas/investor-education/chapter-5-are-lsifs-a-good-choice-for-me/article731366>

Gonick, Cy. 2007. "Gary Doer's Manitoba." *Canadian Dimension*. <canadiandimension. com/articles/1785>

Gonzalez, Juan, Henry Phillips, et al. 2001. *Radicals at Work: An Activist Strategy for Revitalizing the Labor Movement*. Detroit: Solidarity.

Gordon, Todd. 2010. *Imperialist Canada*. Winnipeg: Arbeiter Ring.

_____. 2009. "The Colonial Dynamic in Canada's Economic Crisis." *New Socialist* 66: 39–42.

Gray, Stan. 2009. "Worker Rights."*Montreal Serai*. <montrealserai.com/2009/01/02/worker-rights>

Guard, Julie, Mercedes Steedman and Jorge Garcia-Orgales. 2007. "Organizing the Electronic Sweatshop: Rank and File Participation in Canada's Steel Union." *Labor: Studies in Working-Class History of the Americas* 4, 3: 9–31.

Haiven, Judy. 2007. "Union Response to Pay Equity: A Cautionary Tale." In Gerald Hunt and David Rayside (eds.), *Equity, Diversity, and Canadian Labour*. Toronto: University of Toronto Press.

Hammond, D.N. 2001. "The Gendered Movement Against Bill 147." *New Socialist* 31 (Aug.–Sept.): 14.

Harvey, David. 2005. *A Brief History of Neoliberalism*. Oxford: Oxford University Press.

Heron, Craig. 1996. *The Canadian Labour Movement: A Short History*. Second edition. Toronto: Lorimer.

Herring, Jim. 2002. "Labour, the NDP and Our Communities." <solidaritycaucus. org/?p=25>

Hickey, Robert. 2009. "From Merger to Civil War: Measuring the Cost of Union Infighting." *rabble.ca* July 16. <rabble.ca/news/2009/07/merger-civil-war-measuring-cost-union-infighting>

High, Steven. 2003. *Industrial Sunset: The Making of North America's Rust Belt, 1969–1984*. Toronto: University of Toronto Press.

Hothschild, Arlie Russell. 2007. "Through the Crack of the Time Bind: From Market Management to Family Management." *Anthropology of Work Review* 28, 1: 1–8.

"How Can We Help Build a New Left?" [forum]. 2009. *New Socialist* 66: 30–34.

References

Humphrey, John. 2008. "USW and the Fiasco at Dofasco." *The Bullet* 120 (July 3). <socialistproject.ca/bullet/bullet120.html>

Hunt, Gerald, and Judy Haiven. 2006. "Building Democracy for Women and Sexual Minorities: Union Embrace of Diversity." *Relations Industrielles/Industrial Relations* 61, 4 (Autumn): 666–82.

Hunt, Gerald, and David Rayside (eds.). 2007. *Equity, Diversity, and Canadian Labour*. Toronto: University of Toronto Press.

Hyman, Richard. 1975. *Industrial Relations: A Marxist Introduction*. London: Macmillan.

Incite! Women of Colour Against Violence (eds.). 2007. *The Revolution Will Not Be Funded: Beyond the Non-Profit Industrial Complex*. Cambridge, MA: South End.

ITUC (International Trade Union Confederation). 2007. *Annual Survey of Violations of Trade Union Rights*. <survey07.ituc-csi.org/getcountry.php?IDCountry=CAN&IDLang=EN>

Jackson, Andrew. 2006. "Rowing Against the Tide: The Struggle to Raise Union Density in a Hostile Environment." In Pradeep Kumar and Christopher Schenk (eds.), *Paths to Union Renewal: Canadian Experiences*. Peterborough, ON: Broadview.

_____. 2005. *Work and Labour in Canada: Critical Issues*. Toronto: Canadian Scholar's.

Jackson, Andrew, and Sylvain Schetagne. 2004. "Solidarity Forever? An Analysis of Changes in Union Density." *Just Labour* 4: 53–82.

Jefferys, Steve. 2000. "Western European Trade Unionism at 2000." In Leo Panitch and Colin Leys (eds.), *Socialist Register 2001*. London: Merlin.

Johansson, Mauri, and Timo Partanen. 2004. "Role of Trade Unions in Workplace Health Promotion." In Vicente Navarro and Carles Muntaner (eds.), *Political and Economic Determinants of Population Health and Well-Being: Controversies and Developments*. Amityville, NY: Baywood.

Johnston, Jay. 2008. "Political Relevancy and the Shop Floor." *Relay* 22 (April–June): 12, 50.

Kainer, Jan. 2002. *Cashing in on Pay Equity? Supermarket Restructuring and Gender Equality*. Toronto: Sumach.

Kasser, Tim. 2003. *The High Price of Materialism*. Cambridge, MA: MIT.

Keefer, Tom. 2007. "The Politics of Solidarity: Six Nations, Leadership, and the Settler Left." *Upping the Anti*. <uppingtheanti.org/node/2728>

Kidd, David. 2005. "State of the Unions 2005." *Canadian Dimension* 39, 3 (May-June): 29–32.

Kovel, Joel. 2007. *The Enemy of Nature: The End of Capitalism or the End of the World?* Second edition. London and Winnipeg: Zed and Fernwood Publishing.

Kuhling, Clarice. 2002. "How CUPE 3903 Struck and Won." *Just Labour* 1: 77–85.

Kuhling, Clarice, and Alex Levant. 2006. "Political Deskilling/Reskilling: Flying Squads and the Crisis of Working Class Consciousness/Self-Organization." In Caelie Frampton et al. (eds.), *Sociology for Changing the World*. Halifax: Fernwood Publishing.

Kumar, Pradeep, and Christopher Schenk (eds.). 2006. *Paths to Union Renewal: Canadian Experiences*. Peterborough: Broadview.

Lafrance, Xavier. 2010. "The Battle of York." *New Socialist Webzine*. September 1. <newsocialist.org/index.php?option=com_content&view=article&id=264:the-battle-of-york-&catid=51:analysis&Itemid=98>

Langford, Tom, and Chris Frazer. 2002. "The Cold War and Working-Class Politics in the Coal Mining Communities of the Crowsnest Pass, 1945–1958." *Labour/Le Travail* 49: 43–81.

Lavaca Collective. 2007. *Sin Patrón: Stories from Argentina's Worker-Run Factories*. Chicago: Haymarket.

Lebowitz, Michael A. 2006. "The Needs of Capital Versus the Needs of Human Beings."

Build It Now: Socialism for the Twenty-First Century. New York: Monthly Review.

Leier, Mark. 1990. *Where the Fraser River Flows: The Industrial Workers of the World in British Columbia.* Vancouver: New Star.

Levant, Alex. 2005. "Vote Stacked, Incumbent Wins." *New Socialist* 53 (September–October): 4–5.

Lewchuk, Wayne, and Don Wells. 2006. "When Corporations Substitute for Adversarial Unions: Labour Markets and Human Resource Management at Magna." *Relations Industrielles/Industrial Relations* 61, 4: 639–65.

Lewis, Avi (dir.). 2004. *The Take.* Ottawa: National Film Board of Canada and Barna-Alper.

Lichtenstein, Nelson. 2002. *State of the Union: A Century of American Labor.* Princeton: Princeton University Press.

Lukas, Salome, and Judy Vashti Persad. 2004. *Through the Eyes of Workers of Colour: Linking Struggles for Social Justice.* Toronto: Women Working with Immigrant Women in collaboration with the Toronto and York Region Labour Council.

Luxton, Meg, and June Corman. 2001. *Getting By in Hard Times: Gendered Labour at Home and on the Job.* Toronto: University of Toronto Press.

Lynch, John W., et al. 2000. "Income Inequality and Mortality: Importance to Health of Individual Income, Psychosocial Environment, or Material Conditions." *British Medical Journal* 320 (29 April): 1200–204.

Lynd, Staughton.1992. *Solidarity Unionism: Rebuilding the Labor Movement from Below.* Chicago: Charles H. Kerr.

Lynd, Staughton, and Alice Lynd (eds.). 2000. *The New Rank and File.* Ithaca and London: ILR.

Mason, Paul. 2008. *Live Working or Die Fighting: How the Working Class Went Global.* London: Vintage.

McCreary, Tyler. 2009. "Tough Union, Tough Lessons: Learning from the CUPE 3903 Strike Defeat at York University." *Canadian Dimension* 43, 3 (May-June): 32–33.

McGuckin, Gene. 2010. "Where Is the Union Movement in the Olympic Resistance?" *New Socialist Webzine* February 20. <newsocialist.org/index.php?option=com_content&view=article&id=144:where-is-the-union-movement-in-the-olympic-resistance-&catid=51:analysis&Itemid=98>

McInnis, Peter S. 2002. *Harnessing Labour Confrontation: Shaping the Postwar Settlement in Canada, 1943–1950.* Toronto: University of Toronto Press.

McKeigan, Bruce. 2008. "The Rise and Decline of Local 6500 United Steelworkers of America." In David Leadbeater (ed.), *Mining Town Crisis: Globalization, Labour, and Resistance in Sudbury.* Halifax and Winnipeg: Fernwood Publishing.

McMurtry, John. n.d. "What Is Good? What Is Bad? The Value of all Values across Time, Space and Theories." Forthcoming in John McMurtry (ed.), *Philosophy and World Problems. Encyclopedia of Life Support Systems.* <eolss.net>

_____. 1998. *Unequal Freedoms: The Global Market as an Ethical System.* Toronto: Garamond.

McNally, David. 2010. *Global Slump: The Economics and Politics of Crisis and Resistance.* Oakland: PM Press.

_____. 2009. "From Financial Crisis to World Slump: Accumulation, Financialisation and the Global Slowdown." *Historical Materialism* 17, 2: 35–83.

_____. 2006. *Another World Is Possible: Globalization and Anti-Capitalism.* Second edition. Winnipeg: Arbeiter Ring.

_____. 2000. "Defend OCAP — Solidarity Forever!" *New Socialist* 5, 3 (September–October): 18.

McQuaig, Linda. 2009. "Rich Cause the Crisis, Workers Get the Blame." *TheStar.com* July

16. <thestar.com/comment/columnists/article/665535#Comments>

Meiksins, Peter. 1989. "A Critique of Wright's Theory of Contradictory Class Locations." In Erik Olin Wright (ed.), *The Debate on Classes*. London and New York: Verso.

_____. 1986. "Beyond the Boundary Question." *New Left Review* 157: 101–20.

Miller, David. 2006. "Mayor David Miller Outlines Economic Vision of Toronto's Future." Speech to the Toronto Board of Trade, September 29. <millerformayor.razorbraille.com/speechDetails.php?articleID=605>

Mills, Sean. 2010. *The Empire Within: Postcolonial Thought and Political Activism in Sixties Montreal*. Montreal and Kingston: McGill-Queen's University Press.

Milstein, Cindy. 2010. *Anarchism and Its Aspirations*. Oakland: AK Press and Institute for Anarchist Studies.

Monsebraaten, Laurie. 2009. "Fighting for Dignity on the Job." *TheStar.com* July 11. <thestar.com/article/664487>

Montgomery, David. 1979. *Workers' Control in America*. Cambridge: Cambridge University Press.

Moody, Kim. 2007. *US Labor in Trouble and Transition: The Failure of Reform from Above, the Promise of Revival from Below*. London and New York: Verso.

_____. 1997. *Workers in a Lean World: Unions in the International Economy*. London and New York: Verso.

_____. 1988. *An Injury to All: The Decline of American Unionism*. London and New York: Verso.

Mooney, Ken. 2007. "The Corporate Team Incentive." *Postal Worker* [Vancouver CUPW newsletter] (Spring): 4–5. <cupw-vancouver.org/postalworker/spring2007.pdf>

Moore, Michael. 2009. *Capitalism: A Love Story*. Dog Eat Dog Films.

Moreau, Francois. 1986. "Bilan de l'Extrême Gauche au Québec." *La Gauche*. <lagauche.com/lagauche/spip.php?article1616>

Morissette, Remi, Grant Schellenberg and Anick Johnson. 2005. "Diverging Trends in Unionization." *Perspectives on Labour and Income* 6, 4 (April): 5–12.

Mulholland, Helene. 2004. "Face-Off." guardian.co.uk. <guardian.co.uk/society/2004/oct/27/interviews.politics>

Mulroy, Cathy. 2008. "My View from the Blackened Rocks." In David Leadbeater (ed.), *Mining Town Crisis: Globalization, Labour, and Resistance in Sudbury*. Halifax and Winnipeg: Fernwood Publishing.

Muntaner, Carles, et al. 2004. "Economic Inequality, Working-Class Power, Social Capital, and Cause-Specific Mortality in Wealthy Countries." In Vicente Navarro and Carles Muntaner (ed.), *Political and Economic Determinants of Population Health and Well-Being: Controversies and Developments*. Amityville, NY: Baywood Press.

Naiman, Joanne. 2008. *How Societies Work: Class, Power and Change in a Canadian Context*. Fourth edition. Halifax, NS: Fernwood Publishing.

Navarro, Vicente, and Leiyu Shi. 2002. "The Political Context of Social Inequalities and Health." In Vicente Navarro (ed.), *The Political Economy of Social Inequalities: Consequences for Health and Quality of Life*. Amityville, NY: Baywood.

Navarro, Vicente, et al. 2006. "Politics and Health Outcomes." *The Lancet* 368.9540: 1033–37.

Nelson, Matthew. 2010. "Labour Geography and the 2010 Vancouver Olympics." *Studies in Political Economy* 86: 131–65.

Ng, Winnie. 2009. "PMP Stands for 'Politicize, Mobilize and Power.'" *Labour/Le Travail* 64: 164–67.

Nicol, Janet Mary. 1997. "'Unions Aren't Native': The Muckamuck Restaurant Labour Dispute, Vancouver, BC, 1978–1983." *Labour/Le Travail* 40 (Fall): 235–51.

Niemeijer, Martha. 2004. "Quebec Aluminum Workers Occupy Plant to Stop Closing." *Labor Notes.* <labornotes.org/node/975>

Noonan, Jeff. 2009. "Free Time as a Necessary Condition of Free Life." *Contemporary Political Theory* 8, 4: 377–93.

_____. 2008a. "Normative Political Economy." In Walter R. Levin (ed.), *Political Economy Research Focus.* New York: Nova Science.

_____. 2008b. "The Embodied Good Life: From Aristotle to Life-Ground Ethics." In John McMurtry (ed.), *Philosophy and World Problems.* Encyclopedia of Life Support Systems. <eolss.net>

_____. 2008c. "Reconstructing the Normative Foundations of Socialism." *Socialist Studies/ Études Socialistes* 4, 1: 31–55.

Norton, Wayne, and Tom Langford (eds.). 2002. *A World Apart: The Crowsnest Communities of Alberta and British Columbia.* Kamloops: Plateau.

OCAP (Ontario Coalition Against Poverty). 2009. "Why OCAP Is in Solidarity with City Workers." <update.ocap.ca/node/737>

Offley, Will. 2004. "The P3 Files: Privatization, Profit and Porkchopping." *Canadian Dimension* (May-June). <canadiandimension.com/articles/1968>

Olivera, Oscar. 2009. "For the Reconstitution of the Movements from Below: Autonomy and Independence." *Narco News* December 15. <narconews.com/Issue 63/article3993.html>

Oliveri, Adele. 2003. "Stop That Train!" *Znet.* <zmag.org/znet/viewArticle/10859>

Ostroff, Michael (dir.). 1996. *Memory and Muscle: The Postal Strike of 1965.* Ottawa: CUPW.

Palmer, Bryan D. 2009. *Canada's 1960s: The Ironies of Identity in a Rebellious Era.* Toronto: University of Toronto Press.

_____. 2003. "What's Law Got to Do With It? Historical Considerations on Class Struggle, Boundaries of Constraint, and Capitalist Authority." *Osgoode Hall Law Journal* 41: 465–90.

_____. 1992. *Working-Class Experience: Rethinking the History of Canadian Labour, 1800–1991.* Second edition. Toronto: McClelland and Stewart.

_____. 1987. *Solidarity: The Rise and Fall of an Opposition in British Columbia.* Vancouver: New Star.

Panitch, Leo, and Donald Swartz. 2003. *From Consent to Coercion: The Assault on Trade Union Freedoms.* Third edition. Aurora: Garamond.

Panitch, Leo, and Sam Gindin. 2009. "Transcending Pessimism: Rekindling Socialist Imagination." *The Bullet* 242 (July 28). <socialistproject.ca/bullet/242.php>

Parker, Mike, and Martha Gruelle. 1999. *Democracy is Power: Rebuilding Unions from the Bottom Up.* Detroit: Labor Notes.

Penner, Norman. 1988. *Canadian Communism: The Stalin Years and Beyond.* Toronto: Methuen.

Peterson, Larry. 1981. "The One Big Union in International Perspective: Revolutionary Industrial Unionism, 1900–1925." *Labour/Le Travailleur* 7: 41–66.

Piotte, Jean-Marc. 2009. "Les Victoires des EmployéEs de l'Hôtellerie Québécoise." *À Bâbord!* 28 (February–March). <ababord.org/spip.php?article842>

_____. 2008. "Les Syndicats: Le Dos au Mur." In Francis Dupuis-Déri (ed.), *Québec en Mouvements: Idées et Pratiques Militantes Contemporaines.* Montreal: Lux Éditeur. 97–110.

Pitawanakwat, Brock. 2006. "Red Baiting and Red Herrings." *New Socialist* 58 (Sept.–Oct): 32–33.

Pollack, Marion. 2010. "Embracing the Equity Agenda." *Canadian Dimension* 44, 3 (May–June): 26.

Prashad, Vijay. 2007. *The Darker Nations: A People's History of the Third World.* New York and London: New Press.

Pupo, Norene J., and Mark P. Thomas (eds.). 2010. *Interrogating the New Economy: Restructuring Work in the 21st Century*. Toronto: University of Toronto Press.

Radio-Canada. 2010. "Le SPQ-Libre Expulsé." <radio-canada.ca/nouvelles/ Politique/2010/03/14-SPQ-Libre-expulse.shtml?ref=rss>

Rao, Nathan. 2008. "Election 2008 and Beyond: Radical-Left Strategy in a Time of Right-Wing Consensus and 'Centre-Left' Illusion." *New Socialist Webzine* October 28. <newsocialist.org/index.php?option=com_content&view=article&id=114%3 Aelection-2008-and-beyond-radical-left-strategy-in-a-time-of-right-wing-consensus-and-qcentre-leftq-illusion&Itemid=102>

_____. 2004. "Rise and Fall of the New Politics: Lessons for the Left." *New Socialist* 47 (June–July): 16--17.

Rayside, David, and Fraser Valentine. 2007. "Broadening the Labour Movement's Disability Agenda." In Gerald Hunt and David Rayside (eds.), *Equity, Diversity and Canadian Labour*. Toronto: University of Toronto Press.

Rebick, Judy. 2005. *Ten Thousand Roses: The Making of a Feminist Revolution*. Toronto: Penguin.

Reshef, Yonatan, and Sandra Rastin. 2003. *Unions in the Time of Revolution: Government Restructuring in Alberta and Ontario*. Toronto: University of Toronto Press.

Richardson, Charley. 2008. "Working Alone: The Erosion of Solidarity in Today's Workplace." *New Labor Forum* 17, 3: 69–78.

Rinehart, James. 2006. *The Tyranny of Work: Alienation and the Labour Process*. Fifth edition. Toronto: Thomson-Nelson.

Rosenfeld, Herman. 2009a. "Toronto Labour Council Organizes Stewards' Assembly." *Canadian Dimension* 43, 5 (September–October): 37–38.

_____. 2009b. "The North American Auto Industry in Crisis." *Monthly Review* 61, 2 (June): 19–37.

_____. 2008a. "Challenging the Framework for Concessions." *The Bullet* 153 (November 6). <socialistproject.ca/bullet/bullet153.html>

_____. 2008b. "Class, Labour and Anti-Poverty Struggles." *Relay* 23 (July–September): 36–38.

_____. 2007. "Canadian Auto Workers Surrender Right to Strike, Shop Floor Independence in Magna Agreement." *Labor Notes*. <labornotes.org/node/1450>

Rosenfeld, Herman, and Carlo Fanelli. 2010. "A New Type of Political Organization? The Greater Toronto Workers' Assembly." *The Bullet* 400 (August 6). <socialistproject.ca/bullet/400.php>

Ross, Stephanie. 2009. Interview on *Radio Basics* (CHRY 105.5 FM Toronto) July 27. <radio4all.net/index.php/program/34695>

Ross, Stephanie, and Ron Drouillard. 2009. "Renewing Workers' Struggles in the Crisis: The Windsor Workers' Action Centre." *The Bullet* 228 (June 24). <socialistproject.ca/bullet/bullet228.html>

Rueschemeyer, Dietrich, Evelyne Huber Stephens and John D Stephens. 1992. *Capitalist Development and Democracy*. Chicago: University of Chicago Press.

Russell, Ellen, and Mathieu Dufour. 2007. *Rising Profit Shares, Falling Wage Shares*. Toronto: Canadian Centre for Policy Alternatives.

Ryan, Sarah. 2009. "Organizing in Tough Times." *Briar Patch*.

Saad-Filho, Alfredo, and Deborah Johnston (eds.). 2005. *Neoliberalism: A Critical Reader*. London and Ann Arbor: Pluto.

Salutin, Rick. 2009. "Swallow Self-respect? Er, No Thanks." *Globe and Mail* July 9.

<theglobeandmail.com/news/opinions/swallow-self-respect-er-no-thanks/article1197554/>

Saberi, Parastou, and Stefan Kipfer. 2010. "Rob Ford in Toronto: Why the Ascendancy of Hard-Right Populism in the 2010 Mayoral Election?" *New Socialist Webzine* November 24. <http://newsocialist.org/index.php?option=com_content&view=article&id=314:rob-ford-in-toronto-why-the-ascendancy-of-hard-right-populism-in-the-2010-mayoral-election&carid=51:analysis&Itemid=98>

Saulnier, Christine. 2009. "Curbing Our Enthusiasm: Expectations of an NDP Government in Nova Scotia." *rabble.ca* June 8. <rabble.ca/blogs/bloggers/ems/2009/06/curbing-our-enthusiasm-expectations-ndp-government-nova-scotia>

Sauvé, Roger. 2009. *The Current State of Canadian Family Finances 2008 Report.* Ottawa: Vanier Institute of the Family. <vifamily.ca/library/cft/famfin08.pdf>

Savage, Larry. 2010. "Contemporary Party-Union Relations in Canada." *Labor Studies Journal* 35, 1: 8–26.

Schwartz, Kristin. 2009a. "Filipino-Canadian Solidarity: A Worker to Worker International Exchange." *Our Times* 28, 4 (August–September): 28–34.

_____. 2009b. "Stewards Assembly Makes History." *Stewards Assembly Toronto 2009* [Toronto: TYRLC]: 1–3.

Sears, Alan. 2005. "Creating and Sustaining Communities of Struggle: The Infrastructure of Dissent." *New Socialist* 52 (July–August): 32–33.

_____. 2003. *Retooling the Mind Factory: Education in a Lean State.* Aurora: Garamond.

_____. 2001. "Anti-Capitalism and Canadian Labour." *New Socialist* 30 (June–July): 24–26.

Seccombe, Wally, and D.W. Livingstone. 2000. *"Down to Earth People": Beyond Class Reductionism and Postmodernism.* Aurora: Garamond.

Shalla, Vivian. 2007. "Shifting Temporalities: Economic Restructuring and the Politics of Working Time." In Vivian Shalla and Wallace Clement (eds.), *Work in Tumultuous Times: Critical Perspectives.* Montreal and Kingston: McGill-Queen's University Press.

Shantz, Jeff. 2002. "Solidarity in the Woods: Redwood Summer and Alliances Among Radical Ecology and Timber Workers." *Environments* 30, 3: 79–93.

Sharzer, Greg. 2007. "Only Thing Green Is the Colour of Money." *New Socialist* 62 (Fall): 14–15.

Shniad, Sid. 2010. "The Decline of Organized Labour and How Its Current Trajectory Can Be Reversed." *Labour/Le Travail* 65: 141–48.

_____. 2007. "Neo-Liberalism and Its Impact in the Telecommunications Industry: One Trade Unionist's Perspective." In Catherine McKercher and Vincent Mosco (eds.), *Knowledge Workers in the Information Economy.* Lanham: Lexington.

Silver, Jim. 2010. "Winnipeg's North End: Yesterday and Today." *Canadian Dimension* 44, 1 (January–February): 12–15.

Singer, Daniel. 1999. *Whose Millennium? Theirs or Ours?* New York: Monthly Review.

Slaughter, Jane (ed.). 2005. *A Troublemaker's Handbook 2: How to Fight Back Where You Work — and Win!* Detroit: Labor Notes.

Smith, Doug. 2000. *Consulted to Death: How Canada's Workplace Health and Safety System Fails Workers.* Winnipeg: Arbeiter Ring.

Sobel, David, and Susan Meurer. 1994. *Working at Inglis: The Life and Death of a Canadian Factory.* Toronto: James Lorimer.

Spika, Vera. 2004. "Working Enterprises Provides Labour-Friendly Tax Help." *The Report* 25, 1 (January–February). <hsabc.ca.org>

Stanford, Jim. 2009. "When in Doubt, Blame Unions." *The Progressive Economics Forum.* <progressive-economics.ca/2009/06/29/when-in-doubt-blame-unions/>

_____. 1999. *Labour-Sponsored Funds: Examining the Evidence.* Toronto: CAW Research Department.

Statistics Canada. 2009. "Unionization." *Perspectives on Labour and Income* 10, 8 (August): 27–35. <dsp-psd.pwgsc.gc.ca.proxy2.lib.umanitoba.ca/collection_2009/statcan/75-001-X/75-001-x2009108-eng.pdf>

_____. 2008a. *The Daily.* January 15. <statcan.gc.ca/daily-quotidien/080115/dq080115a-eng.htm>

_____. 2008b. *The Daily.* April 2. <statcan.gc.ca/daily-quotidien/080402/dq080402a-eng.htm>

_____. 2009. [Toronto:] Toronto and York Region Labour Council.

Struthers, James. 1983. *No Fault of Their Own: Unemployment and the Canadian Welfare State 1914–1941.* Toronto: University of Toronto Press.

Tang, Emily. 2004. "Rank and File Union Struggle: Workers at the Metropolitan Hotel in Toronto." *New Socialist* 46 (April–May): 24–25.

Taylor, Jeffery. 2001. *Union Learning: Canadian Labour Education in the Twentieth Century.* Toronto: Thompson Educational Publishing.

Teller, Maggie. 2009. "Common Front Organizing." *New Socialist* 66: 38.

Thomson, Alice, and Rachel Sylvester. 2009. "Class Warrior Bob Crow Claims that We Are All Left-Wingers Now." *Times Online.* <timesonline.co.uk/tol/news/politics/article6831548.ece>

Townson, Monica. 2009. *Women's Poverty and the Recession.* Ottawa: Canadian Centre for Policy Alternatives. <policyalternatives.ca>

Tucker, Eric. 2004. "'Great Expectations' Defeated? The Trajectory of Collective Bargaining Regimes in Canada and the United States Post-NAFTA." *Comparative Labor Law and Policy Journal* 26: 97–150.

Tufts, Steven. 2006. "Renewal from Different Directions: The Case of UNITE-HERE Local 75." In Pradeep Kumar and Christopher Schenk (eds.), *Paths to Union Renewal: Canadian Experiences.* Peterborough, On: Broadview.

TYRLC (Toronto and York Region Labour Council). 2009a. "Message to City Hall: Only a Fair Contract Will Settle the Strike." <labourcouncil.ca>

_____. 2009b. *Stewards Assembly Toronto 2009.* [Toronto: TYRLC].

_____. n.d. [2004]. *Strategic Directions 2004–2010.* <labourcouncil.ca/strategic2004-2010rans.pdf>

Vally, Salim. 2008. "From South Africa to Palestine: Lessons for the New Anti-Apartheid Movement." *Left Turn* 28 (April–May): 26–30.

Vosko, Leah. 2006. "Precarious Employment: Towards an Improved Understanding of Labour Market Insecurity." In Leah F Vosko (ed.), *Precarious Employment: Understanding Labour Market Insecurity in Canada.* Montreal and Kingston: McGill-Queens University Press.

Walkom, Thomas. 2009. "Striking City Workers a Convenient Target." *TheStar.com* June 27. <thestar.com/Article/656836>

Warnock, John. 2005. "The CCF-NDP in Saskatchewan: From Populist Social Democracy to Neoliberalism." In William K. Carroll and R.S. Ratner (eds.), *Challenges and Perils: Social Democracy in Neoliberal Times.* Black Point, NS and Winnipeg: Fernwood Publishing.

Warren, Jean-Phillippe. 2007. *Ils Voulaient Changer Le Monde: Le Militantisme Marxiste-Léniniste au Québec.* Montreal: VLB Éditeur.

Webber, Jeffery R. 2010. *Red October: Left-Indigenous Struggles in Modern Bolivia.* Leiden: Brill.

Weisleder, Barry. 2005. "Advances for International Solidarity at CLC Convention." *Socialist*

Voice. <socialistvoice.wordpress.com/2005/07/03/advances-for-international-solidarity-at-clc-convention/>

White, Ben. 2009. *Israeli Apartheid: A Beginner's Guide.* London and New York: Pluto.

White, Claudia, and Julia Barnett. 2002. "Stage Prop Strategy: Toronto City Workers' Strike." Interview by Paul Lykotrafitis. *New Socialist* 37 (August–September): 26–27.

Wilmot, Sheila. 2009. "Historical Origins and Contemporary Practices of Labour-Community Workers Rights Organizing." Unpublished paper in author's possession.

_____. 2008a. "Workers, Unions, Community and Organizing for Change in Canada and the US." Unpublished paper in author's possession.

_____. 2008b. "Understanding the Social Organization of Labour-Community Workers' Rights Organizing." Unpublished paper in author's possession.

_____. 2005. *Taking Responsibility, Taking Direction: White Anti-Racism in Canada.* Winnipeg: Arbeiter Ring.

Wood, Ellen Meiksins. 1995. *Democracy Against Capitalism: Renewing Historical Materialism.* Cambridge: Cambridge University Press.

Workman, Thom. 2009. *If You're in My Way, I'm Walking: The Assault on Working People Since 1970.* Halifax and Winnipeg: Fernwood Publishing.

Yates, Charlotte. 2008. "Organized Labour in Canadian Politics: Hugging the Middle or Pushing the Margins?" In Miriam Smith (ed.), *Group Politics and Social Movements in Canada.* Peterborough. On: Broadview.

_____. 2007. "Missed Opportunities and Forgotten Futures: Why Union Renewal in Canada Has Stalled." In Craig Phelan (ed.), *Trade Union Revitalization: Trends and Prospects in 34 Countries.* Oxford: Peter Lang.

Yates, Michael D. 2003. *Naming the System: Inequality and Work in the Global Economy.* New York: Monthly Review.

Young, Art. 2009. "BDS Movement Growing: Labour Solidarity With Palestine." *rabble.ca* September 21. <rabble.ca/news/2009/09/bds-movement-growing-labour-solidarity-palestine>

Zerbisias, Antonia. 2009. "Enough Trash Talk About Striking Workers." *TheStar.com* July 15. <thestar.com/article/666245>

Index